9 . h 2h

THE SAVOY BOY

Mise en Place

Michael Moore

Cover photo of Michael Moore © Julia Boggio Studios
Book design by: SWATT Books Ltd

Back Cover: Savoy Boys today – Left to right: John Wood,
Michael Moore, Anton Edelmann, Brian Whiting

Printed in the United Kingdom
First Printing, 2022

ISBN: 978-1-7396771-0-7 (Hardback)
ISBN: 978-1-7396771-1-4 (eBook)

Michael Moore
Suffolk, United Kingdom

www.mooreshowcuisine.com

CONTENTS

Dedication   5

Acknowledgements   7

Foreword   9

Preface: My passion   11

Chapter 1: Causing drama   13

Chapter 2: The pink pinny   21

Chapter 3: Wrong choice   27

Chapter 4: Fulfilling a dream   37

Chapter 5: Frankie Manners   47

Chapter 6: The new boy   55

Chapter 7: The Savoy way   61

Chapter 8: A queen's day   69

Chapter 9: The longest day   81

Chapter 10: Keeping it real   119

Chapter 11: Being black   125

Chapter 12: The old man   131

Chapter 13: Timing and teamwork   135

Chapter 14: Something different   141

Chapter 15: Midnight stars   145

Chapter 16: The new menu   151

Chapter 17: The grip   157

Chapter 18: Make or break time   161

Chapter 19: Savoy, Savoy   169

Chapter 20: After The Savoy   177

Glossary   181

About Michael Moore   185

DEDICATION

To my mum, Mavis Moore – who always believed
in me and never gave up on who I was

Also to Veta Loretta Barrow – my sister, an unfinished story

To Wayne Bosworth, Bossie, who inspired me before I realised how good I could be

and

Ian Moore, the chef, a strong leader in the kitchen

ACKNOWLEDGEMENTS

My thanks to

Anton Edelmann – my mentor, friend and fount of all knowledge

Karen Williams who believed in my story and kept me going as I wrote this book

Sam Pearce who helped me put it all together

Graeme Watson, first a friend and secondly for his great memory

Aubrey Williams, my missing brother who filled in the gaps

Fiona Tanzi Costa for help with many of the pictures

Jamie Bosworth for memories of Wayne

Willie and Ursula Lloyd and Elisabeth Kendal, keen foodies and friends

The late Willie Bauer, the successful secret of the Savoy

Sue Smith, ace at doing puzzles and putting this puzzle together

... and everyone who shared this journey with me

FOREWORD

I n the 1980s, there was quite an aura about working at The Savoy. It was one of three or four hotels in London where young chefs would aspire to work, and I was 29 when I was offered the job as Head Chef. It was exciting times and a very busy place. Anyone who was anybody – royalty, politicians, actors, singers, and well-known chefs – came to eat there. I thought I'd do it for four or five years and it would stand me in good stead. In the end, it kept me busy for 21 years.

I employed Michael Moore in 1984 because he came across as very keen and very serious about his craft. I have always looked for personality and commitment rather than skill. If you are keen enough, willing enough, and young enough, I can mould you in any way I want. So, I thought that there was a good chance of success, and there was.

He's an outgoing man, back then as well as now. You have to make an impact for anyone to be remembered after 35+ years, especially among a team of 120 chefs. He was always good fun, hardworking, with a smile and cheekiness. His heart was in the right place, he gave his best and always went the extra mile. He was popular amongst his colleagues because he was easy to deal with, he was reliable, and he could make a joke when times were tough, and things went south!

There were two things that chefs got from working at The Savoy. If you stayed for long enough, the confidence and skillset you got was quite incredible. You'd learn more than how to cook a few dishes, as at The Savoy, you'd cook in the restaurant, banquets and private parties. You became a very versatile and well-grounded chef who could put their hands to a lot of things. The basic skills acquired over a long period meant that you could pick up a new job somewhere else and run with it.

It also gave you a load of discipline and organisational skills. If you didn't have the discipline, you simply couldn't do the job. Because there was too much to do. Unless you got organised every morning and thought ahead as to what was going to come, you wouldn't have been able to get through the workload.

Michael's commitment and detail to his work and his conduct made it clear very early on that he would succeed in his chosen profession and go all the way. When he came to hand his notice in after 3½ years, and left to go to Germany, he did very well there.

Every time he came back to the UK, he popped in to say hello and tell us what he was doing, so we never forgot him. We were with him every step of his brilliant career, via Berlin, Switzerland, Sweden, Canada etc and the highlight of running his very own restaurant in Marylebone in London, which he ran very successfully for many years.

During his years at The Savoy, Michael worked with some exceptional chefs who, like him, have made it to the very top of our industry and they all remember the cheeky, funny, easy-going fellow who often brought a little sunshine into a very hard and long working day. I'm sure they agree with me that this is why we are all so fond of him and remember him so well!

I thank him for reminding us of the good times and the tough times, and for sharing his experiences by writing this book.

Anton Edelmann,
former Maitre Chef de Cuisiniers at The Savoy Hotel, now retired

PREFACE
MY PASSION

P assion has always been part of my life. As a kid, a fiery temperament and strong belief in myself got me into trouble. As a teenager, my passion for cooking saved me and took me around the world.

I have sacrificed much for this passion, and when I put on my chef's whites, I feel a thrill and creative excitement that no love affair can compete with. But the real journey started at The Savoy.

I was born into a West Indian family, living in the East End of London. We were nine kids. My mother did not have any favourites, but if she had, it would have been me.

I was the baby she almost lost, the eighth child born on the eighth day of the eighth month. Chinese friends have told me that the harmony of my birth position and that specific date is a very lucky omen.

That is not what my mother thought though, as I arrived on the back seat of a black cab, which was speeding towards the hospital. My arrival was two months early and a great worry for Mum – as it was for the cab driver. My first weeks were spent in an incubator but within days I had proved that I had the lungs to make myself heard and the will to survive.

When I was a small baby, Mum used to hitch me to her hip whilst she was cooking and later, as I became too heavy to carry, she would place me on a soft towel in her woven shopping basket, which she placed on the table next to the cooker. My first memories were of the wonderful aroma of West Indian slow-cooked stews and spices such as ginger, cardamon and cinnamon. Mum baked tasty bread with raisins, and I still remember her light but slightly sweet dumplings that she made to go with slow braised pork belly. Dad made a perfect dish of rice mixed with tenderly braised spring cabbage, shredded into fine strips which coloured the rice a minty green.

There is not a day when I don't think of my mother and thank her for the love for good food that she instilled in me, and for teaching me that anything could be achieved with hard work.

I'd like to share my story with you in this book and hope that my journey will inspire you to fulfil your dreams and passions.

Michael

Michael (back, far right) with cousins and brothers, back row from left, Neville and Laurence, and front row from left, Ian, Courtney and Don

CHAPTER 1:
CAUSING DRAMA

My first dream was to be a famous professional actor, as I was mesmerised by the lights of Broadway. And my second dream was to be the best cook in the world.

Well, the first dream was soon put to bed. At school I was a flamboyant little show-off, who liked mucking around and imitating people. I'd be causing drama, making drama, and even taking part in drama. The latter was the part that my teachers enjoyed me doing the most.

This was soon picked up by my drama teacher, Mr Livingston. Sat on his wooden armchair, he would say to me, "Moore! do an impression of a cat."

"Miaow." I would scream like a cat, and he would laugh.

"Do an impression of a fox!" And then I would joke and scratch like a fox. "Go on now, I want you to do a real rough Northerner." And I would put on my Northern accent. Even though it wasn't spot on, he would just chuckle and laugh.

One day he asked me to put my baloney to good use and come to his drama class after school.

When I arrived in the classroom, some of the kids were already chatting to one another. But as I walked in, they seemed more interested in why I was there. A couple of them looked at me and whispered to each other. I was a tough kid – most of them called me Archie, after the famous American boxer whose surname I shared. My reputation preceded me!

Mr Livingston announced that we had a school production of The Wizard of Oz. And after the auditions, where I surprised everyone with my impressions as I delivered the part without a script, he *made* me play the Wicked Witch of the West.

"I'm not playing that, sir, that's a woman's role," I said to him.

"But don't you realise acting is about playing all roles, Master Moore? You can be the best woman there could be."

So, I played the role as the wicked witch. The show ran over three evenings, live in front of our parents. My parents didn't attend though. Very traditional West Indians weren't into that type of stuff.

But nevertheless, I was very excited peeping into the crowd from behind the curtain, seeing faces I knew, other children with their parents. This could be the life I could live. I loved the smell of the greasepaint, and as they applied the make-up to transform me into my character, the excitement started to rise inside. I became a showman and got ready to perform. It was so different from the drab life and difficult time I'd had so far.

The performances went well. We had a standing ovation every single night, especially on the Friday when the hall was full to bursting with parents and children who came to watch the performance. Although I'd joined the drama group with hesitation, it changed me. I had stood on the edges for a while as it felt like all the other kids were clever clogs, but when I took the part, they accepted me, and I became part of their tight-knit family. It gave me confidence and I finally felt like I was one of them and part of something good.

The following Monday morning at school, Mr Livingston pulled me into his office. He said, "You know what Michael, you're quite a character. I think you would do really well at Sylvia Young."

"Who is Sylvia Young, sir?"

"Oh, it's a drama school, they're based in Marylebone." He explained what they did there to develop young people into really good actors, and I got very excited.

But then I bowed my head after he told me how much it would cost. "Yeah well sir, my parents can't afford that, it's a lot of money."

"Yes. But you know we should have a chat with them and see if they would..."

Before I even got home, I knew what the answer would be. With nine children, asking my mum and dad to give me £100 for drama school... with hand-me-downs and lots of mouths to feed, I thought they'd lynch me!

So, I decided not to say anything about it. I went back to school the following day. "Did you have a word with them?" Mr Livingston enquired.

"No sir. Dad was on his way to work, and Mum was busy cooking, but I'll find time." These excuses went on for the whole week until he stopped asking me. Great! He's given up, I thought. He'll leave me alone now.

On the Friday evening after football practice, I walked home with my older brother, Neville, who is a year older than me. And as we approached the front door, I could see this guy talking to my parents. Brown corduroy jacket, grey trousers, thick rimmed glasses, jet black hair, Italian looking, five foot five, not a very tall man. "Neville, is that Mr Livingston?" I asked.

Neville stared at me and raised his eyebrows. "What have you done now? You know man, Daddy's going to be really upset with you."

"I haven't done anything. Why do you always think I've done something?"

"Well, Mr Livingston is one of *your* teachers," he retorted. And he had a point, as I was always the one in trouble and he'd often have to take letters home from the teachers when I'd done something wrong.

I took a big sigh. As I walked towards the door, it opened. I slowed down and paused, whilst Neville slipped past my mother to enter the house.

"How can I help you sir?" I heard her saying.

"Hello, I'm Mr Livingston. I'm Michael Moore's drama and maths teacher."

"Oh! What's he done now?!" was her immediate retort.

"No no no, he hasn't done anything. Well, he has, but nothing bad. I wanted to tell you that he was very good in the drama, he's a talented lad. It was a shame that you couldn't make it to the performances last week, he did extremely well. Did he tell you about it?"

"Yes, he said something, but I'm not really into all that type of stuff."

That's OK. But what I'm trying to say to you is..."

With that my father stepped out from behind my mother. "What do you want?" he asked, expecting the worst.

"Hello, I'm Mr Livingston."

"Yes sir, nice to meet you," my dad responded.

"I was just talking about Michael."

"Him? What has he done now?"

With déjà vu going on, Mr Livingston looked perplexed and confused.

"As I was just saying to your dear wife, he's done nothing wrong. He's an excellent drama student. I was just wondering if I could have a word with you about it?"

"What drama?" my father replied.

"Well, there's a school called Sylvia Young..." At that moment Mr Livingston saw me loitering and looking embarrassed at the end of the path and caught my eye. "There you are! Come in young lad." He grabbed me and put both his hands on my shoulders. "Well? Did you not tell your parents how well you did?"

"Yeah, I did, sir, well, you know..." I mumbled, looking down at the ground, avoiding eye contact.

My father interrupted. "What can I do for you, sir?"

"Well, this young lad has talent. You don't find that every day. Not in these parts anyway you know. There's a school, Sylvia Young, that can develop young lads with their acting and drama."

And with that my father rolled his eyes. "Acting? All he ever does is act up; he doesn't need help with his acting."

My mother was courteous and listened on as my father peeled away from the front door, having lost interest.

"Mrs Moore, all I'm saying is that Michael is extremely talented for his age. And I think that if he went to a school like Sylvia Young's..."

"Does that mean that he would have to leave this school?" she asked.

"No. He could do it after school or at weekends."

"Weekends, weekends, where would he find the time and where's the school and how would I get him there?"

"Well, the school is in Marylebone."

"Marylebone, where's Marylebone?"

"It's in central London," he explained.

"Oh, central London. Well, he's got no purpose to be in central London."

"Well, that's where the school is... But what I'm saying is, the school would develop him into an actor and then once he gets into year 11 and 12, they will subsidise."

My mother lost interest as soon as he said subsidise. "What do you mean subsidise?"

"Well at the moment, you would have to pay."

"Pay? I don't have that kind of money." Without realising how much it was, my mother was on the defensive.

"We don't have that type of money; we have just barely enough food to feed our mouths, and you want me to find money to send him to drama school?"

"Well, it would only cost £100 annually."

"£100?! Where do you think I would find £100?" she spluttered.

With that, my father stepped back into the frame. "£100? For what? Who does he owe money to?"

"No, he doesn't owe anyone any money," my mother replied. "They want £100 to get into drama school."

"I ain't got £100 to send him nowhere. I work too hard all week to be giving £100 away. £100? Do you know what type of money that is?"

"Yes, I do," Mr Livingston responded.

"Look, thank you for your time but he won't be going to any drama school!"

With that they dismissed Mr Livingston. He was left standing at the front door as it shut in our faces. He had a small chat with me, telling me not to give up, and said he would see me on Monday. He got into his Ford Anglia and left.

Awaiting my comeuppance, I heard my father's voice. "YOU! Get in here! Going into school, feeding teachers long stories about drama and acting when you know we ain't got any money."

My father launched into one of his rages and let me have it. "You have nothing else better to do than waste my time to shame this family. Somehow, you're just not like the rest of the kids." And he stormed off.

Ignoring the conversation, my mum shooed me and Neville away to take off our uniforms and put on our home clothes, our scruffy clothes. I thought nothing else about it. I was just happy that my father hadn't taken a swipe at me and tried to keep a low profile.

My mother started to do a little humming and began to cook, so I went and perched myself in the kitchen. Watching her cook, I asked her questions like: Why are you putting that in there? Why are you doing that?

She retorted with a smile. "You ask too many questions." But food was one of my joys; it relaxed me. I loved watching my mother cook – she did it so easily. The exotic Caribbean food she cooked was unlike the food that my fellow classmates would eat. And I'd be quick to take the first taste once it was finished.

She knew exactly how much of each ingredient to put in and when to put it in. And what it was going to taste like. It was fascinating to watch.

From time to time, my mother gave me responsibilities. Not long after this day, there was an afternoon when my mother was working at the hospital, and she had missed the bus on the way home. She phoned our neighbour, as we didn't have a phone. "Mrs Hammond, go next door and tell my son Michael to peel potatoes and get the vegetables ready, but tell him don't touch the fish. I'll do that when I get there."

I was watching cartoons when Mrs Hammond knocked at the door and passed on the message. And as she left, she said, "If you get stuck you give me a shout. Right? And don't peel too much skin off the potatoes, OK?"

"OK, Mrs Hammond." With joy, I jumped up. My father worked nights, so he was still asleep upstairs. I rushed into the kitchen and peeled the potatoes, just how my mother would peel them every other evening. Then I prepared the vegetables, the ones that she'd already left out in brown paper, in exactly the way she'd shown me many times in the past.

And I was so excited about getting it done correctly for her that I put the potatoes on, and I started to cook them slowly; not the veg of course, I knew that much! As my mother came in through the back door she went, "It'll be the death of me, that hospital, the bus driver could see me coming and he drove off, I know that he saw me. Anyway, what are you doing?"

She lifted the pot lid. "Ah, you need a bit more water in there, that's gonna dry out," she said, getting the kettle and pouring in more water. Upon seeing the beans, she said "Good" and went to hang up her coat. She came back, put on her pinny and proceeded to take out the fish, cleaned it, cut it, and then pannéd it in flour. She talked to me as I watched her closely. She asked me, "Why don't you play football with your brothers?"

I looked through the window and saw Neville, my younger brother Ian, and my nephews, thinking they were Pele playing football. I responded, "I would rather be in here with you."

The food was finished and served, and I wanted to get everyone's opinion. "What do you think of the potatoes?" I asked.

My older brother Keith grumpily retorted, "Well, they're potatoes, aren't they? What else do you want us to say?" Then my mother turned around to me and said: "Really nice! Now that you know how to do it, you can do it more often."

I didn't know if that was a sentence or a gift. But I relished the chance to do it again, which I ended up doing very proudly, without being told again.

INGREDIENTS FOR SUCCESS

Making drama or causing drama was never my intention as a child, but having high energy, my mind was always working overtime. This could have easily led me down the wrong road, but other people could see great things ahead for me that I couldn't see. They guided me on the right track, and I will always be grateful to them for thinking of me. This taught me that if you meet the right people in life, they will channel your energy and your ambitions.

So remember, if you also have a state of uncoordinated energy, always look out for the people who give you good advice and can see ahead far better than you can.

CHAPTER 2:
THE PINK PINNY

As we entered year 11, boys were expected to do woodwork and metalwork. And girls did needlework and domestic science, as it was called back in the 1970s. Women were expected to run the home whilst the men went out to work and brought in the money.

I hated the smell of metal, so I protested to my teacher. It was on the same day at the same time that the girls were doing cookery, which I'd glanced at longingly on many occasions as I walked past the doors through which tantalising smells wafted as I went to Religious Education classes.

My metalwork teacher was Mr Smith. 6'4" tall with a beard. And he took no nonsense. He'd often give me a clip round the ear before I'd done anything. When I asked what he'd done that for, he'd reply, "In case you do anything, Moore."

He said, "Young man! What's your problem?" when I protested.

"Sir, I hate doing metalwork. It smells awful and I hate the machines."

"Well young lad, you can sit in a corner and do the theory if you feel that way about it."

"But sir, could I do cookery classes instead?" I asked.

"Cookery classes? Cookery classes? Come now, Archie Moore. Why do you want to do cookery classes, that's what girls do. What would the other boys think of you?"

"I don't really care what they think of me. I just want to do something I enjoy doing, and I like cooking, sir."

"You like cooking? Do you cook at home?" Mr Smith enquired.

"Yeah, I help my mother. You could ask her if you want."

"Really, huh!" With that he looked across the classroom; my brother Neville was there.

"Neville! This scallywag over here says he cooks at home."

"Yeah, he does sir. He helps Mum in the kitchen."

"Wow! So there is a soft side to you then, Archie? Well, lad. I tell you what, you know that my wife is in charge of domestic science across the girls' block?"

"Yes, I do sir," I replied.

"Hahahaha I've got something for you. Come back and see me after the break."

In those days, we had a double lesson with practical first, then a break, and then you would come back and do the theory. Or vice versa. After the first part of the afternoon, I'd lost interest. As we came back to the classroom, Mr Smith called me to one side.

"Moore! Come here lad," he said, and as I walked over to him, he pulled this frilly pink pinny out of his pocket. Asking me to lean forward, he put the pinny over my head, and then turned me around by my shoulders and tied the back. With that, the rest of the class roared with laughter – and so did Mr Smith.

"Right lad, you make your way over to the fifth-year block where domestic science is taking place. I've told my wife, and she's expecting you. The girls have just finished their theory, so it'll be cooking. You'll be calling yourself a little Escoffier! Go on lad, off with you," he said, pushing me out of the door, hoping to humiliate me.

In those days, you had to walk through two playgrounds to get to the fifth-year block. And of course all the classes were taking place. So, as I walked across the playground, other kids stared out of their windows, pointing. I could see a few people giggling, but not giggling too loudly because they knew my reputation. I walked across with my head held high; I didn't really care.

And as I got to the fifth-year block, I observed the world around me. It felt a lot bigger! When I reached the building, I got stopped. "Oi, you! Young lad!" It was Mr Barnes, the deputy headmaster.

"Yes, sir," I replied.

"What the hell are you wearing and where are you off to?" he asked me.

"Um, I've been told to go to the fifth-year block."

"By whom?!"

"Mr Smith."

"Mr Smith?"

"Yes, I'm going to do cookery sir."

"Cookery?! You're going across to the fifth-year block to do cookery?"

"Yes sir. I asked if I could do cookery this afternoon."

"Well lad, you'd better hurry up." And with that, I went, and he gave me a long hard stare as I walked into the shadows.

As I entered the building, I got a waft of the baking that was happening. It smelt so good. Oh my god, what is that, I thought? Mmmmm.

When I got to the classroom, I stood by the glass panelled door. Mrs Smith looked across, saw me hovering in the window and waved a hand for me to come in. She was a short lady, 5'6" small, compared to her husband's great stature. But she was just as aggressive and had a strong voice. "So, you're Master Moore, are you?" she said, stopping and staring at me.

"Yes miss."

"There won't be any scallywagging in here," she said, waving her finger. "I want you to sit right there, right at the back of the class. Have you ever done cookery before?"

"No," I responded.

"So, you'll open your ears then and listen, won't you lad?"

With that, she went to the oven and pulled out this amazing cake. She said, "This is what you'll be attempting to do now, girls and lad. This is called a Victoria sponge. Can any of you explain to me where the term Victoria sponge came from?"

I knew the answer because I'd read it somewhere. But I was a bit scared to say anything. Some of the girls guessed: "Because it was made in Victoria?" and "Because the flour is called Victoria?"

So, I plucked up my courage and said, "I think the cake was made by a cook in honour of Queen Victoria. And it was her favourite cake, so they called it Victoria sponge?"

"That's close enough. Well done. Where did you read that, young lad?"

"I think I read it in a magazine once."

"Well, good for you. You can read! That's correct girls, Master Moore's got it right. It's the Victoria sponge because it was made in honour of Queen Victoria. This cake is created in layers. You take this one sponge, which is about three to four inches thick. And it's sliced into three and then between these slices there is a very thick clotted cream with jam. It's a very simple cake, but it's one of my favourites."

Then she went to the blackboard, and she started writing the recipe so furiously that the chalk crumbled in her hand. "Right. It's now quarter to three. You have until ten to four. This sponge shouldn't take any longer than half an hour tops. Chop chop!" She clapped her hands, signalling to us to start.

We all looked at the blackboard to read the recipe, got our ingredients, which were laid out on the side, and waited for the scales to measure them out.

To the annoyance of Mrs Smith, I started putting the recipe together. It all seemed to come very easily to me. I greased my pan and put the greaseproof paper around it. She came across and looked. "Have you done this before?"

I'd seen my mum make West Indian sponges many times before and although they were different, they followed a similar method. I replied, "My mum always greases the tin at home when she makes cake." And she just walked off!

"Archie, Archie!" I heard a whisper behind me. I looked around and there was this girl, Sharon Smith. "What was the last bit you did? How did you do that?" she asked.

As I started to reply, Mrs Smith looked across and screeched, "No talking in this classroom! I've said it time and time again, get back on with cooking!" Once she'd turned her back, ignoring her I quickly went around the desk and showed Sharon exactly what I'd done. Sharon looked at me with a polite smile and continued.

The ovens were at the front of the classroom. When your cake was ready, you had to take it to the front and Mrs Smith would take it from you and put it into the oven. "Have you put all the ingredients into this, young man?" I replied yes. "Well, we'll soon find out," was her reply.

As the cakes cooked, we were told to write the recipe down in our books, which we did. By the time we'd done that, the cakes were rising. We were called up to the front as Mrs Smith took the sponges out of the oven. She explained the terminology, about cold air, hot air, that sponges would go flat if you opened up the oven too early, and would burn if you opened it too late, and the implications if the temperature was too high. As she took the sponges out she said, "Now all these sponges need to rest."

I kept my eye on firmly on my sponge. I had been left the shabbiest of baking pans. But my sponge sat there proudly, a lovely golden-brown colour, refusing to sink, unlike all the others around it. In fact, it even sat higher than Mrs Smith's sponge that had come out of the oven an hour earlier.

After about another 10 minutes, she instructed us to turn them out. And as we all got our trays and our towels, she showed us what to do. When I flipped my cake, there was a little flopping noise as it released from the baking tin. As it touched the cooling tray I worried that it had broken but when I lifted the tin off, before me was a perfect sponge. Easily three inches thick, sitting perfectly. The girls around me were taking theirs out of their tins, some stuck to the bottom, others lopsided, or a little bit burnt.

I just sat there, very proud, as Mrs Smith walked around. "Oh my god. Is that yours?"

"Yes, miss."

"Are you sure?" Looking from the front, she checked around the classroom to see if I'd taken someone else's cake. But everyone had their sponge. "That's a very good sponge," she said, calling all the girls to my table to have a look.

Prodding the sponge very delicately, she explained to them that it had a lovely texture and height. "All these sponges should have come out like this if you followed the recipe."

It was in that exact moment that I realised I wanted to cook.

INGREDIENTS FOR SUCCESS

I have encountered embarrassment many times when I revealed what I wanted to do as my career. Some people found it a joke and wanted to humiliate me. But I also learnt that their dreams were not mine and they would struggle to understand what journey I was on. I have always taken their negative energy and challenged their thoughts to prove them wrong and show them that my journey is my own.

Never let anyone dampen your spirit or your belief in what you want to do with your life. This takes strength and courage.

CHAPTER 3:
WRONG CHOICE

———————————————

Joining the cookery class after my perfect – and perhaps lucky – Victoria sponge caused a bit of a stir, because they'd never had boys taking cookery before. And if I was a weaker character, I'd probably have quit. But despite the ridicule, most people were happy that I'd found something I enjoyed, and I continued with the class until my schooling ended.

After leaving school, I had some major decisions to make. The dream of being a famous actor, travelling the world, still lingered. But being a chef that everyone adored, creating amazing food, was what I was drawn to do.

They were tough times back then. It was 1978, in Margaret Thatcher's era, and unemployment was high. For most ethnic people it was hard to find work. I would turn up for interviews and as soon as they saw the colour of my skin, they'd either tell you that the vacancy had gone or that they'd changed their mind. I knew what I wanted to do but needed to find a job to get me started.

As I was born in August and left school at 15, a few months before my 16th birthday, I wasn't allowed to work immediately. But I decided to lie about my age so I could get a glimpse of what was going on in the real world.

I was fortunate enough to have family all over London, Suffolk and the Midlands. I went to school in Ipswich (where we had moved when I was small) and spent most of my holidays in East London with my uncle Gordon. As I spent the majority of my childhood growing up in Ipswich, I decided to look for a job around there.

Before I got my first kitchen opportunity, I had a couple of jobs and neither worked out well. I took a roofing job, but I fell through a skylight because I was rubbish at it, and it didn't help that I was scared of heights and would shake as I climbed up and down the ladder. I lasted a week. Then I took on a cleaning job and hated it.

Orwell Park School

So when I saw a job in the paper for 'Kitchen Assistant Wanted: Seeking young person enthusiastic and willing to learn on the job catering for up to 150 to 300 schoolboys', I instantly grasped at it.

The job was in a small village called Nacton, on the outskirts of Ipswich. I got on my bike and rode all the way there for the interview, and it took me a good 45 minutes. Arriving in the village, I saw a beautiful massive old Victorian building at the top of the hill. This was Orwell Park School.

I unclipped my bike clips from the bottom of my suit trousers, conscious of not getting the oil from the chain on them. Locking up my bike out of sight to save embarrassment, I tidied myself up and walked into the school.

Using the staff entrance, feeling it was more appropriate than the front door, I was stopped by a lady who brusquely asked how she could help me. "Umm. I'm here for Mr Angus. For the Kitchen Assistant interview."

As I stood there waiting, I could smell food. I got a glimpse of a small kitchen and this chef with a curly moustache like a German colonel, barking out orders at his small brigade. I could see all the food being put into water basin dishes that were placed underneath warm lamps. This was at around 11.30 in the morning. I was wondering to myself, who eats food at 11.30 in the morning?

Before I could ponder this a tall lady turned up. "Hello, I'm Mrs Angus." I introduced myself and she invited me to follow her. As we walked down the corridor, I could see kids between the ages of five and eleven, neatly dressed and sitting upright at their desks. A far cry from my own schooldays.

Mrs Angus knocked lightly on a door, then opened it. A gentleman was sitting at a desk, and behind him was an amazing panoramic view through the windows of fields that ran right down to the riverfront, the river Orwell. He stood up, surprising me, because he was shorter than me and his wife. "Welcome, I'm Mr Angus, the Head Teacher of the school."

His wife excused herself and left. He told me to sit down and as he finished off scribbling on the page in front of him, he picked up his phone and asked not to be disturbed.

He gave me a background to the school and started to explain the job.

"The position is basically being a kitchen assistant. That means you'll be working with Mrs Green. And Paul Bumstead." He was the executive chef, the guy that I'd glimpsed at the door.

"He has a small brigade. They work Mondays to Fridays. Occasionally we'll work on a Saturday morning. You will be required to work five days a week and maybe sometimes six when we're busy."

And he explained the events that went on within the school while I listened. I was very excited and also very nervous.

He said, "Paul is a very strait-laced man. He likes things to be done thoroughly. But he's a kind gentleman. Do you think you could work with him?"

"Yes sir! I'm sure I could."

"Well without any further ado, let's have a look around." Mr Angus took me around the school and showed me where the boys had lunch, their play areas, their activity sheets. All of this was of very little concern to me. My main interest was what was going on in the kitchen. We eventually arrived there, where he passed me over to the chef.

"You ever worked in a kitchen before?" Paul Bumstead asked me, with a very scrawny voice for such a big man.

I said, "No, no, I've just finished school."

"Oh! So, I want you in here tomorrow morning prompt and early at 7.30. How are you getting here, by the way?"

"Well, I'll be using my bike."

"Where are you living?" he asked.

"I live at my parents' place," I responded, which wasn't exactly true, as I had moved out as soon as I could, but I wanted to make a good impression.

"Well come back 7.30 tomorrow morning, don't be late. When you come in tomorrow morning, Mrs Green will be here."

So after this very short interview, I was offered a job in the kitchen. I cycled away from the interview thinking, this is it, and grateful that I had managed to land a job that was related to food.

The following day, I was up bright and early. I arrived at 6.45am. Mrs Green, who was in charge of keeping the kitchen tidy, was there. She looked a little bit annoyed that I was so early.

"Ah, morning! What are you doing here so early? You don't have to be here for 45 minutes."

I said, "I always like to be early."

She said, "Oh well, you can't get in the kitchen. Paul isn't here yet and we're waiting. I am going to be cleaning outside for a little while."

"I'll give you a hand if you want."

"No, no, no, I'm fine."

So I stood there waiting. Suddenly a car pulled up and I saw the chef get out of it. He looked totally different in his normal clothing than in his chef's whites. He looked up and saw me at the top of the steps to the kitchen. "Morning. Nice and early, that's what I like... Whilst you're standing there, pick up those vegetables and bring them in."

He opened the car door and I lifted up the vegetables and took them in. After I had put them on the table, he directed me to the changing room, where I was allocated a locker. It was shabby, broken, and quite smelly. It didn't have a padlock. So I went back to the kitchen and asked if he had a padlock.

"You have to get your own," he responded, then shuffled through his drawers and chucked me a rusty old padlock. "You can use that one for today but buy yourself a proper one for tomorrow."

I put my clothes in the locker, locked it, and entered the kitchen in a uniform that hung off my small frame. The others were just arriving. Paul said, "Right. There are some pots left from last night. You need to start cleaning them."

Ten minutes later, the young commis chef came in wearing a clean white jacket and walked past me. He said good morning to me and went across to Paul, the chef. They started to have a chat and were laughing together.

The next moment the commis chef came back with a coffee. They stood there chatting and drinking, as I was there trying to get the skirmishes off the pots from the night before. As I continued to scrub away at the pots, some other people arrived. One of them was a shy looking young girl with big brown eyes, very quietly spoken. The Chef walked across and said, "Young man, Michael!" I said, "Yes, Chef?"

He said, "This is the sous chef, Jackie."

"Oh right, nice to meet you."

"Make sure you clean those pots properly," she said. "And make sure you put them there in the right place. OK?"

I said, "Yes, sure, I will." And with that she turned and walked off. Now the three of them were laughing and giggling to themselves. I carried on washing the pots and Mrs Green came over to show me how to rinse them and directed me where to put them.

So I carried on doing as I was told by her, with not much contact with the Chef. I wondered if I'd made the right move. I didn't take this job just to become someone that washed pots all day long. But as the day progressed, with me still washing my pots, I glanced over my shoulder at the food the Chef was making and the people he was organising, and kept one eye on the pots and one eye on the food.

My day finished around 6.30pm. My hands were totally clean and soft from washing and cleaning all day. Not one trace of food to play with – it was a disappointing day.

As I rode home in the dark, I wondered to myself, have I made the right decision...? Well, tomorrow was another day.

****

My routine at Orwell Park School had become very straightforward. I would arrive in the morning and start by washing the pots from the previous day, trying to keep ahead of the Chef. I felt I had learnt very little, that I was being used and was going nowhere. But I had learnt for many years that it was safer to work hard and keep quiet.

I was told by many people during my time there that "this is the way we all started. We all started at the bottom like this". But I wondered how deep the bottom was and how long I would stay there.

One morning, as I arrived, I heard the Chef discussing how unhappy he was with Mark, the apprentice chef. He wasn't turning up for college and the Chef was moaning that the school was wasting its money sending him there. I could hear the Chef was thinking of either letting him go or demoting him. I thought, 'Oh my god, I'm only washing the pots, what if I don't do them very well? I'll be gone.'

Although he never seemed to rate me, the Chef would always thank me for a job well done. But unlike me, he didn't have a passion for food. He was a comfortable chef. He wasn't ambitious or passionate. He loved his job because it was Monday to Friday. He had a joy for his motorbike that he was always talking about when he wasn't cooking. He was like one of the Hairy Bikers, a bit chubby with a twirly moustache which he was training to curl on both sides, and a squeaky voice that he would raise when he was upset.

He wouldn't encourage you to be a chef; it was a convenient job for him. He repeated the same menu every 10 days, and he had no problem doing that. For him it was just a job. Cooking was something that he had to get out of the way so he could go and do something better.

But for me, cooking was everything I wanted to do. Enjoying the taste, the smell, the colours and how we can transform something from the ground into something magnificent; this alone just excited me. I couldn't understand when you became a chef like he was why you weren't excited anymore. Was that how I was going to feel later on in life?

One day I talked to the apprentice, and he told me about the process of going to college and how I could train to be a chef and he gave me the inside track of what I had to do. Although occasionally they'd allow me to cook with Jackie when they were quiet, most of the time I was back in my corner scrubbing my pots.

I'd been at the school for around a year before I finally plucked up the courage to talk to the Chef. It was late one Tuesday afternoon, and the kitchen was pretty quiet.

The Chef was sitting in the corner, doing his weekly order. I had very little to do that day. Most of the boys had gone on an outing, and there weren't many people on the premises. So I took my chance, and I went over to him. I said, "Chef, could I go to college? You know, they start back again in September, and I would love to go."

His instant reply was, "We don't have the budget to send two of you to college. And if you want to go to college, you will have to go on one of your days off."

"I don't mind that, Chef."

"Yes, well like I said already, we don't have the money or the budget in the kitchen to send two of you to college."

A few days later, I took it upon myself to go to the college and followed the big signs that said 'ENROL', so that I could find out more. I skimmed through the information listed and found 'Catering 7061/02: September – Apply Now'. I walked nervously up to the desk and told the receptionist that I was looking to enrol. She asked me about my work and where I was working. "I work at Orwell Park School," I said with a stutter. She went down her list. "We already have a young lad here from Orwell Park School. You're not down here with him."

"No, because I want to pay for it myself," I replied.

"Pay for it yourself?!" she asked. "Does your boss know about this?"

"Yes, I asked him, he said I would have to basically come on my day off and pay for it myself."

"This is going to cost you £87."

"To enrol?" I gasped.

"Yes, to enrol," she replied.

£87 sounds very little today, but back then it was a hell of a lot of money. My shoulders dropped. I left despondent, taking the application form with me but with very little hope that I'd be filling it out.

Back at the school the following day, Jackie the sous chef came up to me. "Are you alright today, Michael? You seem very quiet." I dismissed her questioning, telling her I was fine. But she wasn't convinced.

Later, she approached me again. "What's wrong? You can tell me you know; Paul can be a bit of a bugger. Some days he gets on all of our nerves."

I told her about my predicament. "No, it isn't Chef, I just want to go to college. I didn't leave school to be a pot washer. I want to do something with my life."

She responded, "Yeah well you know doing this job isn't always fun. I mean look at the hours that we work. We all arrive here around 7.30 in the morning, and we don't leave until about 5.30 or 6 o'clock. That's a long day."

Little did I know that later on in life this would be like a holiday camp to me. At that moment, I said, "I don't mind the hours. I just want to learn something and coming to work and washing pots every day, I'm not learning everything. I try to watch what you and Paul do, but it's no good if I don't get the chance." Talking about the apprentice, I said, "He takes very little interest in what he does, but yet he's the apprentice, I don't get it."

"Oh, don't you worry too much about him. Just focus on what you're doing, just keep your head down. But if you need to do this, and you want to go to college, you know they're not going to pay you more money here."

I said, "I need to find another job, something that I can do, something so that I can go to college."

She said, "It's the only way out. You could speak to Mr Angus."

So I took it upon myself, and met with Mr Angus. Not surprisingly, he told me the same thing that Paul had told me earlier. "We don't have that type of money to inject into our kitchen. It's a very basic straightforward kitchen, as you've noticed, Mr Moore. I'm very happy that you're interested in going to college, but why don't you wait till next year? Maybe when the apprentice moves on, the position will become open and it could be yours."

I couldn't see myself being here another year washing pots. I had to do something about it. When I got home that evening I thought long and hard. What could I do? How could I get to college? I only had until 12th September to enrol. I had to do something about it.

INGREDIENTS FOR SUCCESS

Sometimes what you're seeking isn't staring you in the face. It hides behind less interesting prospects and you take on jobs that are not your first choice. For me, especially during a time of high unemployment, the job at the school felt like my only option. I took it with the intention that it would lead me to where I wanted to go. And it did.

So, you need to have patience. Sometimes you will take a longer route to get to where you want to go, but eventually it will lead to the place you really want to be. Not every step is forward; some are sideways and some of them are occasionally backwards, but you will achieve your destination if you are patient, believe in yourself and take the opportunities that are presented to you.

CHAPTER 4:
FULFILLING
A DREAM

I made the decision to fund my first year at college. But affording it was a struggle. I asked at the school for extra work, but there was nothing available. I did manage to get an evening job working in a pub that served food. That meant I'd leave the school and then work at the pub until 11pm. But this gave me enough money to put aside for the first year's enrolment fee. I was determined not to give up on my dream of becoming a chef.

It came around to September and I started my studies at the college. I remember walking down a corridor on the first day, my chef whites on and my necktie in my hand along with my hat. All of a sudden, I was confronted by this big beefy looking man, Mr Barnes, one of the lecturers.

"Don't you respect your uniform, young man?" he asked me. I looked surprised and nodded. "Well, why are you walking down a corridor without your necktie on? Get out. Go back to the changing room and dress like a chef. You will not walk down the corridors looking like some scally off the street."

"Yes, Chef," I said and ran back to the changing rooms where I found a couple of other students. None of us knew how to do a neck knot. We accosted a guy who walked in wearing a necktie and asked him. He took his off, and he demonstrated to all three of us. "This is how you do your necktie and make sure you tuck it in at the bottom; the Chef hates any neckties that are sticking out."

As we walked down the corridor with our neckties on, Mr Barnes looked at us again, raised his head and then looked the other way.

We raced to the class and queued outside the nominated classrooms. Five minutes later, a tall, slim man with a chisel-like beard walked towards us with his chef's hat on, in his precise, clean whites. He smiled.

"Morning. Morning. I'm Pat Wright, I'm your lecturer, come in." We followed him in. "Find yourself a place to sit. This is the place I expect to find you every week when you're in my class."

I landed up sitting next to a guy called Tim, a small guy who I'd often see dressed in a leather jacket. I later discovered he was obsessed with the band U2. We said hi to each other and agreed to share the bench.

Mr Wright gave us details about the layout of the college and told us where catering would take place, on the fifth floor.

He said, "This floor is unique; it was only built two years ago. As you see you have a panoramic view of the whole town from here. You're very lucky to have windows all around you. In this year's course, we will do theory in the morning and practical in the afternoon."

We would always have to repeat the dish that we'd done at college during our week at work and we'd have to get proof of this from our head chefs. So we knew the arrangement. I thought this was the beginning; this was something unique. I was going to become the chef I wanted to be. I never doubted myself.

But as my little mind wandered, I was rudely interrupted by Mr Wright. "Are you paying attention, young man, there?" I apologised. "You seem to be in a little world of your own, would you like to share?"

"No sir, I'm sorry." And with that, Pat Wright gave me a look with his warm eyes, and he carried on chatting to us. He had this way of always having a bit of flirtation with the girls to make them laugh and feel comfortable – harmless behaviour. But he knew exactly how to make people relax. And he would always affirm what we did, saying things like "That's good" and "Make sure you do it like that again".

As the year went past, the tips and the knowledge we were picking up from this man were astounding. He was more than a lecturer; he would tell stories in between classes of his days at the five-star Royal Garden Hotel.

"When you work in a five-star hotel, it is vital that you get things right and consistent. And that is why you're all here. I am teaching you all how to do these dishes, and you have to teach yourselves how to be consistent. This will mould who you are." And he would always bring this into play when we were doing dishes. "Don't hurry them. Do it properly."

I formed a very good bond with Mr Wright. He was always there for my questions, and I had a thousand questions to ask about everything. I was very interested in what was going on and in his opinion.

One day he said, "The French are meant to be the dictators of food, but we're not far behind them now." He then blurted out, "Do you know who Escoffier is?" And of course I did, because I had taken it upon myself to read a lot of books about these chefs.

"Yes, sir, I've got my hand up."

"Don't shout it out, young lad, I've told you before, put your hand up. Right. What were you saying, Moore?"

"Escoffier is a French chef, and he came to Britain."

"And what hotel did he work at?"

"The Savoy, Chef, The Savoy."

Pat Wright trying to sort out the mess made by his young trainees. A great teacher at showing you how to get things done

"What have I told you about shouting out? Well, anyway, he was the one that created the kitchens in the format that we have today in two sections." And then he explained all the departments, and what the positions meant. He said, "At the top is the executive chef, and only he sits in the office, and he dictates what's going on. And then there's the head chef, who's on the floor, and he dictates what happens on the floor. And then he has sous chefs. What is the sous chef? We had this discussion two weeks ago."

Tim raised his hand. "A sous chef is like a supervisor. He makes sure that the chefs below him are doing exactly what's required."

Pat Wright (centre) with colleagues

And then Mr Wright went on to explain the role of the chef de partie, the chef of department, and that a department could be anything from fish to meat and vegetables.

Then he talked about commis chefs. "A commis chef is just the slave of a kitchen," he told us. "You are instructed to do whatever is required of you. And at the moment you guys are not even commis chefs. You're all apprentices, so that means basically you don't have a say whatsoever. You just do as you're told."

Understanding this gave me the ambition that I wanted to make it all the way to the top. I wanted to be that executive chef, the one that sits in their office, the one that writes the famous menus and recipes. How much fun that would be, and how proud my parents would be. Once again, Archie Moore was daydreaming...

From the moment I met Pat Wright I knew that I was in safe hands. He was a funny teacher, but he knew where the line was drawn. He would never ever step over it and he would not expect you to, and you instantly had respect for him.

By the June, I felt like I had built a friendship with Pat, and we are still friends today. I'd often go in during my time off and have a chat with him. He started to encourage me to find work in a great hotel or good restaurant. I had always wanted to work somewhere where I could cook great food, and he introduced me to some of the best hotels.

He would often tell me stories about his time at the Royal Garden Hotel, the amazing food they produced and what they cooked for certain people, and the most exciting bit was about the brigade. How they had big brigades and they cooked food that you could daydream about.

One of our first lessons was producing fresh tomato soup. I had only ever eaten tomato soup from a tin, never made it fresh. He gave us the recipe and we did the theory. Then after we had a break, we proceeded to cook the soup. I remember putting all the ingredients together exactly, to copy how he had done it. The bacon, the tomato paste, the hint of flour, all the ingredients that went into making it and letting it cook out.

I wanted to get this so right. And I don't know if it was luck or if I was just a good student, but when it came to Mr Wright trying all of our soups at the end of the day, when I presented my soup and he tried it he suddenly stopped. He said, "Right, what's in that?"

I still remember this day and have jokes with him about it even now. I was confused and he said to me, "This soup you've made is so good there's got to be a tin somewhere." He even looked in the bin and around the kitchen for it. It was only later that I realised he was joking. He told me that the soup was absolutely divine, and he invited the other students to try it.

"The colour is perfect, it's got a nice shiny glaze, it tastes amazing," he said. "This is because you've cooked it out right and you've done it properly." I felt like I was 10 feet tall that day. From that moment I felt that Pat Wright realised I wanted to do more than I was doing. I used to turn up at his classes earlier only because I wanted to learn. It was the day of the week that I knew I was going to learn. He was so easy to listen to and explained everything to you. He wanted every one of his students to do well and that encouraged me as the weeks went on.

****

One day, as I was working at the school, a friend of the Chef's arrived. He was a really good chef. He looked like he'd come from somewhere special, and he was baking cakes in our kitchen. He giggled with Paul who carried on with his normal daily chores. I asked the Chef who he was, and he said, "Oh he's a friend of mine, he works in London."

I said, "Oh, I'm from London, what part of London is he from?"

"He's from White City. Do you know White City?" Yes, I did.

"When he comes up here, he does some stuff for a function round here once in a while. I allow him to work in the kitchen. Anyway, haven't you got any pots to be washing? Standing here, wasting my time..."

"Sorry Chef." And as I went back to work I could see this guy cooking so gracefully and making these amazing desserts. I didn't realise at the time that he was a patissier, a pastry chef. He was doing it so elegantly, and everything he did, he did with such precision. And I thought – wow!

I was so happy he was there for those few days. One afternoon, he started chatting to me. "So young fella, what are you doing here?"

I said, "I work with Mrs Green; I help out in the kitchen and do the pots."

"You shouldn't be wasting your time doing that – a young fella like you. You should be doing more exciting things; you should let the old people do that, that's why they're all here. Why don't you get yourself into a good hotel?" he suggested.

"Hotel?" I asked.

"Yes, that's where most of the apprentices are; they go to good hotels, they get jobs there. I know one of the owners at a really good hotel across the other side of town. A guy called Ian Hatfield. He was looking for some young chefs."

"Really?!"

"Yeah, really, I'll put a word in for you. I'll be back next Thursday. I'll see what I can do," and with that he went. That afternoon, I polished every single pot until it gleamed, excitedly thinking about the possibilities.

The days went by with the same routine. I couldn't wait. When the following Thursday came along, I saw his big shiny motorbike pulling up outside. And as he came up, he said, "Alright Paulie, how are you doing?" They embraced one another and started giggling and laughing and chatting about his bike. Since Chef also had a bike they chatted away for 20 minutes.

I thought he'd forgotten all about me, so I put my head down and carried on washing my pots. He waited for the right moment when Paul wasn't in the kitchen, and he approached me. "Oi you! Archie."

"Yes?"

"I spoke to that fella, Ian Hatfield, and he is looking for a young guy. You need to get in touch with this chef. He's called Frankie Manners."

That name seemed familiar. And I racked my brains and realised that I knew him from a jazz club where we both hung out from time to time.

As this was in the days before mobile phones, I took it on myself to ride my bike from the school around six miles to the other side of Ipswich to Belstead Brook where Frankie was the head chef. The hotel was tucked away in a corner of this large town.

Approaching up the gravel driveway I got a view of the beautiful grounds, and was greeted by three peacocks standing on the front lawn screaming, hurting my ears. Once again embarrassed of my poor old bike, I left it by a hedge, and walked up towards the hotel. I saw the staff entrance so I walked to the back where a lovely shiny red car was parked.

The next second a guy came running out towards the car, fully aproned in a chef's jacket with a chef's hat in his hand. I stopped in my stride. He turned, looked at me and went, "What do you want? What are *you* doing here?"

"Hi Frankie," I replied.

"Michael Moore, oh my god, what are you doing over here?"

I said, "I didn't know you were a chef."

He told me that he had been a chef there for three years. He asked me about what I was doing, and I told him that I was working at Orwell School, although I added a little white lie and told him I was a commis chef in the kitchen.

"Oh, you work at a canteen?!" he asked.

"No!" I frowned with annoyance. "No! The food is quite good."

"What are you doing here?" he asked me again.

I said, "Well, I spoke to this guy, and he knows your boss, and he told me that you had a vacancy."

"Oh yeah, I didn't know that it was you he was talking about. We're looking for a new chef to join us; the guy in the kitchen is leaving at the end of next month. We need someone to replace him. It's a commis chef position."

I said, "Oh great, fantastic, can I see your kitchen?"

"Of course! Just let me get my stuff out of the car." And with that, he grabbed what he had gone to the car for and led me in.

Following him in, I could see this kitchen was a totally different design than the one I was working in. There were about eight chefs, all working in different areas, all cooking different things.

There was an area where the pots were done. But no one like bossy Mrs Green, just a guy with his head down, scrubbing away in blue overalls. Everybody else was dressed in chefs' uniforms, and they addressed Frankie as 'Chef'. And that made me buzz – them all calling him 'Chef' all day long. They didn't call each other by their names here. It was fascinating.

He showed me around and addressed the chefs as he did so. "This is the guy that does the fish, and this guy does the entremetier. Make sure you cut those baton carrots the same size, I have to tell you every evening." He turned around and said, "Those two girls over there, they work on the pastry." There was a glass wall behind which two girls were cocooned in the corner creating pastries, sweet foods, colourful foods. And then he said, "This is where I am, I'm on saucier. This guy working next to me, he's Selwin, he thinks he knows it all", and they had a giggle with one another. Then he asked Selwin to show me around, which he did with a big grin from ear to ear as he explained how everything worked.

I noticed this guy that was working on veg, whom I said hello to. He introduced himself as David. "Don't worry, I won't be here much longer, I'm moving on." Putting two and two together, I realised it was him who was leaving.

As I was shown around the kitchen, they started plating food and it was like watching a painting being carefully created. The Chef was precise in how he cooked everything, and he would shout out to the others, "Bring me the vegetables, bring me the salads, make sure there's not too much salt on those vegetables, that's great, that's not so great."

He would plate up the food, and then he would call out "Service!" Waiters would walk in and take the plates into the restaurant. I stood in the corner of the 'pass', the area where all the food was presented underneath white heated lamps which shone down on the stainless-steel surface. And Frankie would scream out, "These lamps aren't here to keep the food warm all night long, they're just here for seconds. I don't want the food cooking under these lamps so hurry up and get it up here when I call for it. How many more times have I got to tell you, David? When I call a table away, you've got to be up here!"

"Yes, Chef." And with that, they carried on like a clean cog at work. The machine was working. Frankie offered me the position there and then. "You want to work here? Would you like this position?"

"I don't know, because I'm still at the other job, but I could come in the evenings after work. I could get here for around 7 o'clock."

"That'd be fine. If you get here at seven then you can work with David, and he can show you how the vegetable section works."

I said, "Oh, that'd be great." Now that solved my problem. I would have a part-time job at the pub, a full-time job and extra money to pay for my second year at college.

I realised that my time at Orwell Park was coming to an end. It had been a learning curve and very tough. My hands were probably the softest hands in the whole of Britain.

INGREDIENTS FOR SUCCESS

I've always been a dreamer and dreaming is good. It inspires you and as a young man, it gave me the energy to do better. I'd fulfil one dream and it led to the next. It inspired me; it made me think of better things and how to do things that I thought were out of reach.

Even today I still dream, and it pushes me forward. No job or project is too big, so if there's one thing you can learn it's that being a dreamer can make you a more positive person.

If you believe in something, go for it. If you are a dreamer, dream big!

CHAPTER 5:
FRANKIE MANNERS

<hr>

For the next month I continued to ride my bike from one side of the city to the other every morning, five miles to the school, six miles to the hotel and then another five miles home whilst I worked my notice. But I was really excited to spread my wings and learn more.

I enjoyed my work at Belstead Brook, and one of the things that made the hotel different was that the whole kitchen brigade was black, which is unusual now, let alone back in the early 1980s. Ian Hatfield didn't see colour.

During the course of the year, Frankie supported me at college. Although he had already nominated two chefs to go to college that year, one of them hadn't turned up so he gave me the space.

Within a few weeks, once I was settling into the Belstead Brook and getting used to how it worked, Frankie was always praising me. "You're doing a great job, Michael. Oh my god, you're so creative with your food, the vegetables are so much better than David's."

I felt sorry for David during his last few days. He would say, "This is how I always wanted you to do it, David. But you were never interested. Good job, Michael", although I would always tell David how we did a good job together. When David left, I was a little bit nervous. "How am I going to survive on a Saturday night?" I had done many Saturday nights without David, but for some reason, knowing that he wasn't going to be there any more on Monday morning made me wonder how I was going to cope. But I loved working under pressure. It became one of my strengths. So as Saturday night would loom, the Chef would be screaming out, "Make sure everything is ready for tomorrow night! You know, we're going to be doing over 100 covers. I don't want us to come in on Saturday and find we are prepping all day for Saturday evening."

Belstead Brook hotel

I would have Saturday morning off, as it was quiet, although that meant I missed serving breakfast to the local football team, Ipswich Town. I would turn up around 3 o'clock, and just get on with making sure everything was totally ready for the evening. The evening would go fast because they were so busy. But I always had this joy, because I was always ready and ahead of it. I was so far ahead that it meant I could help others out, which meant I could learn more, and they appreciated the help.

It made me a strong member of the kitchen, and I enjoyed being recognised early on in my career. Frankie was always teaching me things. He was the first chef to ever show me how to make a tomato rose. Back in those days, the plates were decorated with a tomato rose with snips of parsley as the leaves. He would decorate a plate and stand back to admire his work. His meat would be cooked to perfection. The fish was always crispy.

And he would always say, "That's what you call cooking" and he and Selwin would compete as if they were on two different teams, but you knew they were one in the kitchen that night and they both would cook away. And I would make sure that my vegetables shone on their plates as well as their main courses. One of the things I loved about Belstead Brook and Frankie's influence is that he always encouraged me to practise what I'd learnt at college and would give me feedback on what I'd cooked.

A year went by and suddenly I realised that the end of college was getting nearer. Mr Wright would remind us that we had to do well. He would say that if we finished with the qualification in our hands, we could work at The Savoy. Those were his exact words, no other hotel. Even though he had worked at the Royal Garden and spoke about this all the time, it was The Savoy's name that rolled off his lips.

I asked him about this one day and he told me that he'd never worked at The Savoy, but it was an amazing hotel, probably the best in London. He told me that he had heard about things that they did, and they had a famous chef. I asked him about the Royal Garden. He told me that it was a great hotel, but not to waste my qualification there.

The Belstead Brook team

He seemed to focus on a few of us who he thought would go all the way, not in a horrible way towards the others, but because he knew which of us were going to take these exams and take them further, so he would spend his time chatting with us and passing on his ideas. I was happy to be one of them.

I was getting itchy feet just after I had sat my exams at college, and Mr Wright asked me how I thought I had done. I thought I'd done well, and he agreed. Theory was always more difficult, and I would hover over the questions because they looked too easy.

I finished the exams and then I decided that it was time to move on from Belstead Brook. It was time to go back to the big smoke. I started applying for jobs back in London, focusing on the five-star hotels. Every week, I would get a letter regretting that there were no vacancies, so I began to think it would never happen.

As summer came and the college was closing, Mr Wright called me to see what was happening. I told him about my plight and that I wasn't having much luck. He reminded me to keep it up and that my luck would change.

I woke up one Saturday morning and there on the floor by the front door were three letters. Picking them up, I could see the stamp marks printed on them. One said The

Hyde Park Hotel, one said The Grosvenor House, and the third one was stamped The Savoy Hotel. My heart almost stopped. I could accept it if the other hotels refused me, but The Savoy Hotel's letter was the one I had been waiting for.

I grabbed the letters and without hesitation jumped on my bike and rode down to the college, knowing that on that particular Saturday morning Mr Wright was going to be there. He took other courses that fell outside his usual work calendar.

I burst into the room. He was preparing for a class and was surprised to see me. I blurted out "I've got three letters", puffing and out of breath. He didn't seem to be surprised as I'd had letters before, and they had all been rejections. He asked me to open them up, but I was too nervous. He asked me why these. "One is from The Savoy, sir."

I pulled up a chair nearby and sat next to his desk. He took the letters and opened up the first one. He read it. "Congratulations, you have a job at The Hyde Park Hotel if you want it!" I was excited and punched the air. At last, it was happening, I thought, instantly forgetting the other two letters. He reminded me to wait for a moment. He opened up the second letter, from The Grosvenor House, who had offered me a job as well. By that stage I was confused about which one to take.

He opened the last letter. It was thick creamy paper. I could just see the watermark as he read the letter silently to himself and then he looked at me. He leant forward, picked up the other two letters and tossed them into the bin. He said, "You can go to The Savoy, they want to have an interview with you." They hadn't offered me a job like the other two hotels, but they wanted an interview with me.

I couldn't believe that he had put the other two in the bin. It was just a gesture, but I was instantly nervous. Mr Wright reassured me. "Just be yourself and go to the interview."

I remember that interview well. I was confused as I stood in front of the hotel because the cars were entering from the wrong side of the road. It's actually the only road in Britain where you can drive on the right due to the tight turn as you approach the hotel.

As I arrived at the entrance, a gentleman in a tall hat looked at me and asked if he could help me. I told him I was there for an interview, and he asked me to go through the Simpson's entrance, down the steps to the Human Resources department.

When I entered, I was approached by a lady and told her that I was there for an interview. After 10 minutes, a gentleman met me and introduced himself as David Louth, the Human Resources manager, and he invited me to follow him into the kitchen to meet the chef. We went down a long narrow hallway and then a tall man in chef's whites approached me. With a strong south German accent, he introduced himself as Anton Edelmann, the executive chef.

We exchanged pleasantries. He asked if I had worked in a hotel like this before and I said I hadn't. It was very busy. Everyone wore hats that made them look so tall and an apron that went from their hips right down to the floor. This is how real chefs dress, I thought. After explaining about the refurbishment, with many chefs working in temporary kitchens, he took me into the main kitchen, and I'll never forget that moment.

When he walked through the kitchen, everyone was at work and as he passed them, they greeted him like a god. "Hello Chef", "Morning Chef". These guys were walking up with bowls and spoons, and he would stop and taste them, and he would tell them: "Too much salt" or "That one needs more salt" or "That one is too creamy, do it again". He had a comment for everything. I stood there watching the chefs approach him one after the other. The one thing that stood out is that they all wore these jackets and embroidered in dark blue writing on the left side of the chest was 'The Savoy'.

'I want one of those jackets' was all that was going through my head.

I realised that when you work in a hotel like this, you would get to cook with all the ingredients you could dream of – like lobster and saffron. You name it, all the ingredients were there. I stared as he told me how they produced everything from scratch. Moving around them, I could see all the chefs lined up in the pass, where the food would be presented, and they were all responding in turn "Yes Chef". And I jumped as they did so.

The Chef said it was a very busy kitchen and asked if I could cope. I said that I could. He invited me to follow him to the other side of the kitchen, where some chefs were assembling hors d'oeuvres, while others were in the potage and the larder, the cold kitchen where all the prep is done for cold dishes, afternoon tea and platters.

He introduced me to two chaps, Victor and Maurice, in the food production area. Victor was the butcher. He dealt with all the red meat that came into the building. The carcasses would arrive, and Victor would prep them down into portion size. Watching this gentleman work was like watching a classical musician; he knew exactly what he was doing. He spoke Italian with broken English but with respect for the Chef, who was half his age. Maurice dealt with everything that was poultry or birdlike and they worked opposite each other.

You would think they got on like a house on fire but in fact they were always arguing and bickering. They were always at it and acted like a couple of old ladies, as I discovered later on.

From there the Chef took me to the quietest part of the kitchen, the pastry department, and introduced me to a man with a George Michael shadow beard who seemed like he was mumbling. After leaving me there for a while, Anton Edelmann came back and took me upstairs. He told me that they had 16 sous chefs, 50 chefs de partie and 50 commis chefs.

I was offered the job there and then. He told me that I would start as second commis chef in the section called hors d'oeuvres, and that's where I started at The Savoy.

Mr Wright was pleased. I was nervous as I was still waiting for my exam results and knew they wouldn't give me a contract if I had failed them.

I also had to tell Frankie that I had a new job. Everything was coming at me at once, but nothing could stop me from having the biggest smile on my face. It was a tough decision. After my shift, I asked if I could have a word with him. As I sat in his office, it was like he could read my mind. He just looked at me and said, "When do you want to leave?" It was like he already knew. I told him about my job at The Savoy and although I could see sorrow in his eyes, he congratulated me and told me how pleased he was for me.

I had passed my exams, was leaving the area I lived in and was going to London to start the dream that I had always wanted. I was about to become a Savoy Boy!

INGREDIENTS FOR SUCCESS

_____

In most of our lives there is a person you come across who is ahead of you and who looks like your own dream of the future. For me this was Frankie Manners who epitomised everything that I was dreaming and thinking of. These people enter your life for a reason. Most of them will guide you because they see a little bit of themselves in you and vice versa, so they enchant and embrace you and lead you forward.

Frankie was the person that led me to my first real serious relationship with food. His inspiration and energy encouraged me to do better. It was as if he knew that I was on a journey. So, listen eagerly because these people will come along in your life, and they will catch your ear. There are many Frankie Manners out there; you just have to know who they are.

CHAPTER 6:
THE NEW BOY

I t was a bright sunny day that I arrived at The Savoy. I was so familiar with London already, but WC2, the West End, was like the big city. I remember it very well. It was a very early morning. I was up at six, and the sun was already sitting high in the sky – a glorious welcome for me in the first week of July 1984.

I didn't know what to expect. I was nervous and hadn't slept well the night before. I'd only recently settled into my digs and started to get familiar with the area over the weekend. And suddenly Monday was upon me.

I navigated my way into central London from Turnpike Lane. I got off at Covent Garden, took a sharp right and meandered through the crowds in the early morning market, making my way down to the Strand.

I arrived outside the Strand and looked straight across to see a pub. Funny name for a pub – the Coal Hole – I thought. And lodged right next door to it was a theatre – the Savoy Theatre. Wow, they had a theatre too!

Directed to the workers' entrance at the back of the building by a friendly concierge, I walked through little tunnels. People were coming and going even that early in the morning. I walked up to the timekeeper who was waiting for arrivals, and told him that I was starting today. He looked down at his piece of paper, confirmed this and directed me to Human Resources.

As I made my way up through the narrow corridors, I started seeing other lost people, also starting on the same day as me. I bumped into one particular guy with a very thick Scottish accent, very friendly, who was waiting outside the personnel department. I introduced myself: "Hi, I'm Michael Moore. Are you a chef?"

"No! Never in a thousand years. I'm John Laing. I'm here as a commis waiter."

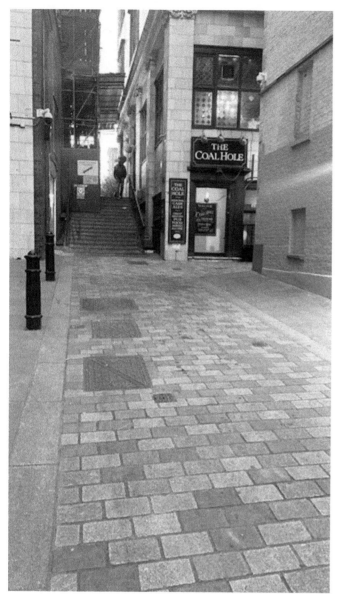

The Coal Hole pub

We waited together, making small talk, and were soon joined by a third fellow who introduced himself as Noel Murphy. He had a strong Irish name but a Brummy accent, and was also going to be working in the kitchen. Mid conversation, David Louth, the Head of Human Resources who I'd met during my interview, invited us into his office.

We all filed into this very narrow room where three or four people were already sitting. Mr Louth, a short man in a nice crisp suit, looked up at us. He said, "Gentlemen, this is The Savoy Hotel. This morning, you will be shown around the whole hotel. So your appearance has got to be correct, because we will be going into public areas."

I was excited. This was one of the world's best hotels, and now I was going to get a chance to see around it. We were hustled away with a few others who joined our crew, and we were led through to the front of the house, as it was known, which included all the client and customer areas. Anything to do with the staff was called the back of house. These were all new words to me in the catering business, and it was like they had their own language. We ended up in the reception area. We were all clustered around Mr Louth who told us to huddle close together and he lowered his voice.

"This is the reception. Such stars as Frank Sinatra, Bing Crosby, Bob Hope, Julie Andrews, and Liza Minnelli have all graced these reception areas. And we make sure that The Savoy has the standards to maintain that."

The carpet beneath my feet was like a cushion. It was soft, fluffy, an amazingly dark red colour. As I looked around, I could see the concierge and receptionists all perfectly dressed. We were taken around and briefly introduced to people who weren't busy and given a brief explanation of the areas and what happened there. At the time the hotel was managed by Willie Bauer who we met, followed by his personal assistant, Deyon Johnson. Unusually she was a lady of colour, and there weren't many of us working in the hotel.

We whizzed through the hotel looking at private rooms, guest rooms, even back of house areas that I didn't know existed, including a place they called the 'plonge' which is French for where you clean the pots and pans. And then it got to the crème de la crème, I think for at least two of us – myself and Noel. Our ears pricked up as soon as we heard the clatter of pans in the kitchen.

As we looked up, we could see what looked like thousands of chefs walking around busy, no time to give you eye contact. You had to stand out of their way because they would just walk right through you. But everyone parted when the Chef walked in. There he was, Anton Edelmann, standing in his glory in the most spectacular clean whites in the middle of the kitchen. I later found out that the men in tall, starched hats around him were sous chefs, listening as he shouted out the orders and directed them.

As we walked into the kitchen, we caught his eye, and he came over. Mr Edelmann was a man of control and he wanted to know who we were straight away. He looked at me. "Oh, Mr Moore, how are you?" He had remembered my name and I greeted him back.

"Hello, Chef. Morning. I'm fine. Thank you."

And then he turned and said the same thing to Noel. "How are you, young man? How was your journey into London?"

Noel replied with his Brummy accent, "Great Chef, great."

And then Chef asked, "So are you staying with us now?" With that, David Louth released us to his care and left us.

Everyone called Mr Edelmann 'Chef'. You wouldn't hear his name. Asking us to follow him, he introduced us to another chef, Heinrich, who was blonde, about 5ft 7", also German. I thought kitchens were meant to be full of French people, but all the seniors were German.

Before I could introduce myself, a voice came from behind me, "Get out of the way, get out of the way" in a strong French accent.

"Morning Dominique. How are you?" the Chef asked. Dominique replied, expressing his misery about another hard shitty day ahead and saying that they were two men down.

Heinrich looked at me and he said brusquely, "You, young man. Go and get changed. You're going to be working in hors d'oeuvres." I was led away by one of the commis chefs to the changing room, leaving Noel alone with the Chef and Dominique.

We chatted on the way. He told me how long the days were and asked me where I came from and why I wanted to join The Savoy. And I asked him, "Are they always so direct?"

He replied, "Heinrich isn't so bad, but don't get on the wrong side of Dominique. You know, he's not the happiest chef here."

I gathered the chef's whites that had been given to me earlier and put them on. The trousers were big, and the jacket was... well, it drowned me, but I was proud as monkeys that it had 'The Savoy' written on it.

He showed me how to put the apron on and to forget about what I had learnt elsewhere. There was a Savoy way. So, I watched what he did, copied it and put on the apron. He said, "Maybe in a couple of weeks' time, if you're still here, you'll buy a chain for your apron because those strings tend to pop quite easily so it's best to get a bit of chain and thread through it. Then it won't pop."

He led me back to the kitchen, in my squeaky clean chef's whites. I walked into the kitchen, thinking that I would be noticed and they would all cheer and say "He's arrived!", but nothing happened. I just blended into the rest of the chefs that were there – it was strange. I thought people would start asking me who I was, what my name was. My first instruction was, "You over there! Don't just stand there dawdling, get across here. I need these melons ready for service. You know how to prep a melon?"

"Yes. How would you like it prepared, chef?" I replied, stuttering.

"You don't know how to do a bloody melon for fuck's sake." Oooh he swore at me!

"I want you to do them this way. You pick up the melon, squeeze it, smell it. You press the bottom, you press the top and if they're too ripe, you just put them back in the box. We'll send them back. The bastard suppliers never get it right anyway." Then he picked up a second melon. "This one's firm."

He started making a star shape on the top of the melon, pushing the knife left and right through it until he pulled from the top and brought out the star shape. "Right, use these small spoons because you don't want to damage it, and you scrape out all the insides. And once you've done that, we're going to put a little bit of port in them and you're gonna put the lid back on and put them in that fridge. You get me?"

I said, "Yeah alright chef."

"There's a box over there with about 30 of them. When I come back in 15 minutes they'd better be done."

So I made the space and started to work. A second later, a young girl came up to me and said, "Oi, what are you fucking doing now? I'm working there."

I explained that I had been asked to do the melon and she replied, "Don't give me shit newbie, just get on with it right?" I found out later that this girl was called Suzanne. She was probably the smallest lady in the kitchen, but very aggressive indeed. So, I just put my head down and started to prepare the melons.

I heard some chefs gossiping away in the background, making remarks under their breath: "How long do you reckon he's gonna last?" "What, the newbie? I tell you what, I bet you that you do the potatoes later on that he'll only last two days." "What about the one over there?" "Oh, well he's not gonna last a week." "And what about that Scottish kid?" "Ah, well, I don't know about him!"

I realised they were talking about all the new chefs that had just arrived. It was fun for them; it was a bet. The loser would do the prep, peel potatoes or any other task that the winner would ask them to do.

No one made conversation with us; they just left us to get on with it. It was like code red to speak to the 'newbie'. And you could always tell the newbie, because they'd be the one with a badge with their name and position on it, but they never lasted long as they'd break, fall apart or you'd lose them.

As the week went on, and I started to blend in, and I was proving that I could keep up with them, one guy came up to me. "Hi," he goes, "you're new, aren't you? Where you from?" I told him briefly. "Oh, I know East London. I used to have a mate that used to live over there." He had this very strong country accent. He said, "I'm from Bristol." I told him I had never been. He said, "It's a nice city, nicer than this fucking shithole. Anyway, keep your head down."

And there we were – I realised I was now a Savoy chef.

All the 'glam' had suddenly gone and I was just a worker. I felt like I was just a number. What had happened to all that fantasy of working in the famous Savoy?

INGREDIENTS FOR SUCCESS

———————————————

Being the new kid in any establishment is an advantage. You walk in knowing very little but come out the other end with knowledge. I have always been excited upon starting a new chapter in my life, especially in the kitchen. The Savoy kitchen is still today one of the biggest chapters in my life that I have ever experienced. I was a good little chef when I walked in there, and felt absolutely hopeless after my first day, but the excitement that I was going to learn to become better encouraged me.

So, remember being a new boy or girl will always be an advantage; have your honeymoon and enjoy it. It helps you to get on your feet and absorb the knowledge that's being thrown at you.

CHAPTER 7:
THE SAVOY WAY

When I started working at The Savoy, the Chef had asked me where I wanted to work, and I was adamant that I wanted to work on fish. He said to me, "I tell you what Michael. Give me two months on hors d'oeuvres, and then I'll put you on fish." So I agreed.

Six or seven weeks in, the Chef came to me and said, "Michael, come with me." He plucked me out of the section and walked me across the kitchen. As we were walking down the corridor, I thought, 'Ooh, he's going to put me on hot fish' but we walked straight past it. As I looked back confused, he walked me through the butchery and larder, and then he said, "Morning Simon, this is Michael. He'll be working with you from tomorrow."

Unfortunately, this wasn't hot fish, it was the cold fish section. Hot fish is where all the glamour takes place. You make the food look amazing and cold fish is where you do all the prepping of the fish ready to be cooked. I realised my mistake. Although a couple of weeks later, when another chef left, I became the first commis of the section working under Simon Reeves, the chef de partie, which made the move worthwhile.

Across the hotel, we were a brigade of around 120 chefs and there were typically 85 to 90 chefs in the kitchen on a normal working day, although it did depend on the season. It was a tough kitchen. But unlike other chefs who arrived and left weekly because they didn't like hard work, I was lasting the course, despite other chefs thinking I might not make it. When it looked like you were going to stick around, the other chefs made the time to get to know you. But only once they felt like you were one of them.

I started to remember names and make new friends and get to know the different characters: those who were serious, others who were funny and some who were strange! Chefs in a professional kitchen can be very temperamental, and it was an intense, high-pressure environment. Everyone had their own way of doing things and while some worked very well there were others that didn't work well for you. It was like walking on stepping stones; you had to be very careful of how you approached everyone, well that's how it felt to me, especially in the early days with my limited experience. But you had to remember everyone's little foibles, and woe betide you if you got it wrong.

Certain leaders stood out in every department. People like Wayne 'Bossie' Bosworth, a small chap, slender and with a fringe that covered his eyes. He was a lively fella; wherever he was in the kitchen you could hear his voice laughing, bossing and joking. Wayne was someone that everybody in the kitchen loved. He had his expression for lads who couldn't keep up or the new kids; he would always call them 'soft'. No malice, of course, it was just a form of identification. Whatever name Wayne gave you it seemed to stick, and everyone would follow suit.

If you wanted to know anything that was going on in the kitchen, you'd talk to Bossie. He always wanted to know what everyone was doing. Sometimes I didn't know what section he was working on; one minute he was in hot fish, the next in larder, then potage. He was like a hummingbird collecting honey ideas for his next dish. Chef gave him that freedom because he noticed that he could work with all of us. I was fascinated by the way Wayne worked. He would do things with food that I didn't understand. It was like he came from a different decade ahead of time, with ideas for food creation that no one else had seen before.

There were a lot of lads that kept that kitchen together, like Stuart McLeod, Aubrey Williams, Julian Marshall, Dave Sharland; the list goes on. The Chef knew that there were many nights and days when we would be very busy, and these guys would stand up and be counted. I always gauge myself on being as tough and as strong as those lads and I think that's what brings progress in your own standards and work.

There were people I got on with really well outside of work. As Noel and I started on the same day, our friendship bonded from then and it wasn't long before I started sharing a house with him and John Laing, the Scottish waiter that I also met on my first day. We moved into a three-bedroomed house in Turnpike Lane, because it worked out cheaper and it was on a direct route to the hotel. I became good friends with Aubrey Williams and John Wood. It wasn't like we would always go out after work for a drink, but occasionally we would meet up in the Coal Hole pub outside the hotel. And it *was* like a coal hole, dark and dingy, but it was ideal for us; we could stay for a lock-in and a couple of jars.

I would not always go because I was not a heavy drinker and plus, they couldn't stand the smell coming off me from the fish. Imagine walking past a fish market on a really hot day when the fish is about to turn. That was the smell that I had on me every day. At 6.30 in the morning, the fish would arrive at the back door. Three-foot-wide polystyrene boxes would have about ten whole salmon in them, packed in ice. I'd have four or five of these boxes stacked high which I'd have to gut. Then my jacket would dry, and the smell would follow me all day. We were told to wash with lemon, and I bought three bottles of citrus shampoo, but they did nothing. I couldn't smell it anymore but everyone else could. It didn't matter what I wore or how many times I showered; the smell of the cold fish would linger. A bit embarrassing but it did ensure that I would get a good seat on the tube home every night!

Anyway, back to the lads. John Wood was a lot quieter than most of the other chefs, and a similar height to me with fair hair. He was known for his comments. Everything he noted, he would talk about, but in a nice way. He would laugh, his right eyebrow would rise, and his facial expressions meant that you could always tell what he was thinking.

Aubrey Williams was driven. He always wanted to know what was going on, was always ready for action and hated people taking shortcuts. You would hear him getting upset with guys who wouldn't listen to the way it was. Aubrey was a smaller guy, but he was fearsome.

There were also a few girls in the kitchen, but not that many. There was little Sue who worked on potage and hot fish, and she held her own against the lads. Then there was Rosemary who worked on the roast, an Irish lady with her hat always tilted to one side. She always looked like she was going at dinner lady speed but she got the job done and you could hear her voice screaming above the boys when she had demands from her section.

It's fair to say that most of the other girls were situated in the cold kitchen or the pastry, as it was biased in those days towards the main kitchen being for boys. Working as a girl in a professional kitchen, there was no excuse that a pot was too heavy, that it was too hot; you were expected to do the same job as the boys. For example, if a pot was too heavy, we would just drag it along the floor or ask one of the kitchen porters to give us a hand. But I didn't think the lads even noticed the gender of the chef, as long as the job got done.

The kitchen was brutally hot and especially when all the stoves were fired up for service. An hour in, you could see the sweat just pouring off everyone. I think the sous chefs must have had special air conditioning built into themselves because they would stand on the pass in their perfectly clean whites. No sweat, clean aprons, pristine jackets and shouting loudly for what they needed to fulfil the orders.

The Chef would always appear from his office just as service was starting and go straight to the mike and scream out a special order. Everything was read out in French in those days, and he would get a resounding "Yes Chef" straight off. Sometimes I didn't understand, and if we got it or not, we just said "Yes Chef", rather than annoy him, and then we'd sneakily ask the sous chef for the order again. We knew what was going on most of the time!

After we had the new kitchen, which I talk about in the next chapter, my section was connected to the front of the kitchen through a microphone, and I would leave the microphone on so I could hear the whole service. In cold fish, not only would we be preparing food that would be served cold such as mousses and caviar, but we also prepared the fish that was going to be cooked in the hot fish section, as well as co-ordinating with other departments to deliver our food. It was also useful to know ahead of time what they were running short of, as I would keep an eye on the numbers that we had available for service.

One of the first things that we learnt at The Savoy was how important it was to be in the right place at the right time. There is a place for everything and a flow to the way food is prepared and the Chef always has his eye on you! Kitchens can be dangerous places so there was no room for mistakes. That is why the hierarchy is so important; teach and learn and get it right first time. The Savoy kitchens were huge and were divided into stations that were responsible for preparing different dishes, hot or cold, fish or meat.

We worked in teams or 'brigades' and within each brigade there were leaders and a descending level of experience ending with the first commis – the starting point for an aspiring chef. Mind you, the most important team members are really the KPs – the kitchen porters – we couldn't have done our job without them.

The executive chef is the boss, the conductor of the orchestra, and the head chef translates their wishes. The senior sous chef oversees the chefs in their sections and the sous chefs next in line are like the wasps in the nest running around supervising so that the chef de partie who is the head of the department can work with the rest of the brigade ensuring the work gets done under the watchful eyes of all of those above – especially the 'Chef'.

In a way the chefs de partie controlled the kitchen. They would be the first to know if anything was changing or anything was happening in the kitchen on the professional front, and they knew how to get revenge on other sections that would mess with them, so you had to watch your back if you upset them too often. Alan Maw was one of them. He would come down to the cold fish section and put a tray of his beloved garnishes in the top of my fridge; of course he would be polite enough to ask my permission, but he would do it anyway and this was his way of hiding things that he didn't want others to get hold of. The kitchen was very demanding, and everybody was after what they needed to get through the day. I totally understood that as I was a little bit like that myself; it saved you time and energy on so many evenings. Pots, pans or ladles even, I would lock up in one of my fridges with a padlock so they would be there the next morning when I arrived so I wouldn't have to go scouting in the kitchen for them. It all seems a little bit evil and harsh, but it was just the way it was when you needed to get things done and you'd do anything to get ahead.

Hygiene was really emphasised. There was no place for making the customer unwell from sloppy practices in the kitchen. Keep raw food away from cooked, hot from cold and so on. I learnt early on that proper preparation was everything. The 'mise en place' meant that cooking could become a joy and an art if everything was properly prepared. We would spend months in different sections, and it could quickly become apparent where our skills lay.

Some chefs became experts all around the kitchen and these talented chefs were known as chefs tournants as they could be called upon to go anywhere as needed. Every section had its professional name. Hors d'oeuvres or starters, the rôtisseur (roasts), the vegetable section is known as entremetier, the larder is the cold kitchen and yes you have guessed it boucherie is where the butchery is done. Fish is divided into poisonnier froid (cold fish) and poisonnier for the hot fish. The potage section is where the soups, noodles and pasta were made. The saucier is for another skilled art, making sauces. The patisserie at The Savoy was a very special section, and the most amazing creations came out of there.

The different sections in the kitchen supported the à la carte menu and also banqueting. Most of our profit from the food delivery of the hotel came from banqueting. It was often said that the kitchen was the show, and the banqueting was for the dough.

Everything that banqueting did made money, because unlike à la carte where you had less control over what people would eat and the numbers of covers you would serve, in banqueting you would have your numbers and know how much money you would make per head. Banqueting could probably take in three large parties in one week what the restaurant would take in a month.

Andrew Jordan, or Mr Jordan as he was referred to, was the head sous chef in banqueting. Tall with blonde hair pulled to the side, strong blue eyes and a very sturdy mean look, he took no nonsense. He was always directional about what he wanted, and he was sarcastic after almost every sentence. But if you did a good job, he would thank you.

He would walk around the kitchen with his clipboard, approaching every section looking at the ingredients or the dishes that he needed for certain parties.

Not much of a people pleaser, he would ask for what he needed, and then he would want you to bring it to him. The banqueting kitchens were very slim and narrow with salamanders at either end to slightly reheat the food before it was sent out. The holding ovens were hot, very hot; it was still one of the oldest parts of the kitchen though you would have thought that this room would have been given greater importance as the part of the hotel that did so many banquets.

He didn't have the elements he needed to be very organised in sending the food out, but Mr Jordan made it work. I'm still amazed today how he managed to send out so much food from this area, shuffling around the chefs who would be screaming and sweating but yet everything went out perfectly.

One particular morning, he came into the cold fish section to speak to Simon, the chef de partie, about a fish platter that we were preparing for 180 people for lunch. After he left, Simon instructed me to create the plates. It was a medley consisting of a rose of smoked salmon, prawns, Marie Rose crevettes and fish terrine. That's four different elements x 180 plates, and we'd make our Marie Rose sauce from scratch (often 40 litres of it) so a big task for the smallest department in the kitchen!

It was the first big job that Simon had trusted me to take on my own. Although we had pre-prepared most of the items, it was left was to me to plate it perfectly, and to have been given the privilege of doing that meant that Simon trusted me. He knew I didn't need supervision and told me to set my plates up on one side. Because of the lack of space we would divide the plates into a row of 10, three deep, making up the numbers of places that were required.

Simon completed the first plate and we discussed it and then I continued plating the other 179 plates. At the time that was a big ask but I was always keen to learn and impress. The plates were then placed onto a holding trolley that could take up to 200 plates at a time. Each plate would have its own stand and all the plates were put on there with precision.

I used some cling film to wrap round the upright trolley from top to bottom and then wheeled the trolley down to banqueting closer to service time.

This was the funny thing about The Savoy: every section of the kitchen was involved in banqueting in some format. Even though we had a banqueting finishing off kitchen, it was all the sections from the main kitchen that prepared each course, so you could quite imagine the pressure on the kitchen on a busy service of à la carte and room service, when banqueting requested that each section provide the course for them. Especially when there were three or four different parties going on at the same time.

Some days it felt like a tsunami. There was a lot of work to do!

INGREDIENTS FOR SUCCESS

The Savoy way showed me the standards that would remain with me for my whole career. They used to say "the Savoy way or the highway", meaning if you didn't do it their way there was no future for you in their house, but they lived up to it very well because their standards were extremely high. I am not saying that other hotels were not just as good, but you knew that if those standards were implanted into your head, they would stay with you for a long time after you'd left The Savoy.

So, when your standards are high, maintain them regardless of what is happening around you. You will always know when you are working somewhere that isn't up to your standards and you'll either improve them or you will move on. The Savoy way carried me all of my career.

CHAPTER 8:
A QUEEN'S DAY

When I started at The Savoy, we were working in a temporary kitchen whilst a new kitchen was being constructed. Space was at a premium and yet the volume of work was still the same. If the old kitchen had been difficult for the chefs, the temporary kitchen was even more of a challenge with pots on the floor making it like an obstacle course.

When we got the new kitchen that we had all been waiting for, it was like the transition from driving an old banger to a bright gleaming Rolls Royce! Our equipment could be properly lined up on the walls in front of us, the heat wasn't as fierce, and although we had teething problems, we worked them out. It was a dream.

Alongside state-of-the-art equipment, natural daylight flowed through the kitchen, and it was one of the few hotels with kitchens to have this, which was a bonus considering the long hours we worked and the fact that we often didn't see the daylight. It was situated on the second floor, whereas most kitchens are in the basement or lower floors.

The Chef had an office which was staged higher than the kitchen, which meant that he could sit there and look over us. Having an intercom on his desk meant that he could get through to any department, including those which were hidden around the corner.

The main kitchen was all under one roof serving all the hot food from the rotisserie, potage, saucier and poissonier. And then we had another department to the side, which was the larder and the cold fish, which made sense as it was attached to the back of the kitchen (the coolest part) and then the butchery. The pastry kitchen was located in the basement. The pass, where all the food was presented and completed before being sent out to the restaurant, was 30 metres of gleaming stainless steel.

Sous chefs on parade for the Queen Mother - Barry Colenso, Andrew Jordan, Garry Hollihead and Calum Matherson. Chef Anton Edelmann is on the left.

The chefs were all keen and eager to get going to try it out. As for me, well my new cold fish section had been allocated a corner position and a window with real daylight and I had my own walk-in fridge. Maybe I had been put in the corner because of the fish smell but I was happy. The whole kitchen was streamlined, bright and shining clean with white tiles decorated with a blue sliver.

And Willie Bauer was proud of the new kitchen. It was a show kitchen. It had a beautiful corridor right down the middle, where he would show guests the state-of-the-art facilities and walk through without interfering with the chefs. Willie would show them around and through the kitchen and around the whole hotel as he was incredibly proud of what he and Anton had created.

Around three months after we moved into the new kitchen, there were whispers of an official opening. In reality, it was the last thing that we needed. We were getting used to new sections and a new layout. But when we heard that a member of the royal household was going to open the kitchen, we felt differently.

True to the Chinese whispers, one day we were gathered in the main ballroom along with the waiters and back of house staff. Standing in front of us were Willie Bauer,

The Queen Mother in the new boucherie with Chef (far left) and Victor and Maurice (both far right in their chef's whites), while Willie Bauer (next to them) looks on.

Chef and Mr Shepherd (the deputy manager), and they announced that the new kitchens were going to be blessed and opened by Her Majesty Queen Elizabeth, the Queen Mother. This sent shockwaves of excitement through the ballroom. We now had less than two weeks to be ready for this special day, a queen's day.

I must say I was really excited. I'd never met anyone famous and on top of that the royal family. What would my mother think? My head was racing with excitement along with the rest of the lads and girls. I was definitely going to make sure I didn't miss this, even though the Chef said he wanted us all to attend even if we were on our day off.

The day of the Queen Mother's visit was like any normal day. We arrived early and had most of our prep sorted and ready. The atmosphere in the kitchen was a little bit strange, more of an atmosphere of excitement. Service had become secondary although we knew the Queen Mother was going to be walking round the kitchen in the afternoon, so we were hoping the lunch would be quick and prompt.

We spent the morning cleaning and keeping the sections tidy. We were issued with new clean jackets with a pink napkin that we were going to use as our neckties. We

The Queen Mother at the opening of the new kitchens with Stuart McLeod (far left), Martin shaking her hand, and Chef and Willie Bauer looking on

had all been drilled in what we should do and how to behave. I think it was the first time I had cleaned my boots to make sure they were presentable, in case Her Majesty glanced at my feet!

By 1.30pm, lunch was coming to an end, unlike the usual when it felt like it went on forever. As I made my way down to the changing rooms to get changed into my new jacket, I'd never seen it this busy. We shared a few jokes and as soon as we were ready, we went back up the stairs one by one and were told by the Chef to go to our sections and await further instructions.

When eventually the Chef came through to the larder and cold fish sections and told us he wanted us all to line up along the route of the kitchen, we all jostled for position as there was no particular order that he wanted us all to be in.

The sous chef came along the line to check our neckties. We had never worn these before and they were a little bit short. Pink was the Savoy colour which connected us to the royal family. Most of us succeeded in doing the famous Savoy knot, and those that struggled were helped out promptly.

We were then briefed by the Chef: Only speak when you're spoken to by the Queen Mother or any of her entourage and if she does speak to you, you will respond with 'Yes ma'am' or 'No ma'am', and nothing else unless you elaborate.

The conversation was repeated right down the line as there were easily 60 to 70 chefs that had turned up for this unique day. After waiting 10 to 15 minutes, we heard a commotion coming down the corridor. The Queen Mother had arrived and I could hear Willie Bauer, the Chef and the rest of the entourage in the distance.

They started from the cold fish section and made their way along the line, which ended at the hot kitchen. I was placed just at the entrance of cold fish. As she walked past us, the Chef introduced her to the sections. She looked at us one by one, shaking hands, occasionally pausing to speak to a random chef. Unfortunately on this day I wasn't one of the lucky ones to be picked for a conversation, but I was still very happy to be there and meet her.

The Queen Mother was a delightful, pleasant lady, softly spoken and totally elegant. I've never been this close to anyone royal in my life. This was fate and an everlasting memory and all I could think about was what my mother would say later when I told her I met the Queen Mother and shook her hand. Once again, the grand old lady Savoy had given me a first to remember. This had me on a high for the rest of the day, in fact for the rest of the week. Photographs had been taken by the press photographer and I wondered if I was in any of them. I did find out later on that I wasn't, but the memory is still here with me today as one of my greatest moments.

After the Queen Mother had left the kitchen, everyone was buzzing, claiming that the Queen Mother had spoken to them. Even the sous chef was chatting amongst the boys about it. Excitement was soon brought to a halt with Heinrich screaming out that new orders had come, and normal service would resume. The chefs that had come in on their day off soon departed as quickly as they had arrived to avoid getting caught up in doing an evening service. I had been there from early doors, and I still had a few things to do before I would leave. I didn't get out until around 8 o'clock that evening and that would be my 13 or so hours for the day, but I didn't mind because the joy of meeting the Queen Mother kept me on a high for the rest of my shift.

THE QUEEN MOTHER
TOURS THE SAVOY

KITCHEN REMODEL - 1986

The old kitchen being broken down

A serving trolley sits alone and abandoned in the old kitchen

Temporary kitchen and plate washing area. The monster of a dishwasher did 200 plates every three minutes.

The new kitchen

Lindon gets to grips in the first few weeks of the new kitchens

INGREDIENTS FOR SUCCESS

This experience was one of the most memorable during my time at The Savoy. Although we knew we did a good job, to have all of us assembled together and for our skills and abilities to be recognised was something else entirely, especially as we were praised in such a formal manner by a most wonderful and famous royal legend.

The lesson I learnt from this is to be proud of what you do and allow others to say thank you.

CHAPTER 9:
THE LONGEST DAY

During my interview for The Savoy, Anton Edelmann asked me if I had a girlfriend, which I thought was a strange question at the time. He said "Michael, you have a choice, is it the hotel or your girlfriend?" I chose the hotel, despite having a beautiful girlfriend and being besotted about her, and I soon found out why he asked me this question.

Some days could be extremely long and extremely busy. The lads would turn up most mornings a good couple of hours before they were meant to be there, depending how much they had to do. We would discuss this whilst we were getting changed. Some of the chefs de partie would be barking at their commis chefs in the changing rooms, telling them what they expected of them and what they needed them to do for the day.

As I was preparing for many of the other chefs by providing cold fish for other departments, I always had to be ahead of them, and I was prepping for the day after and the day after that. I would be calm, cool and collected but this spirit never lasted long because out of the blue, like a big surprise, once you arrived in the main kitchen the sous chefs would be hustling around you telling you that parties had changed, numbers had gone up, and certain dishes were no longer on the menus because the Chef had decided the menus were now going to be different.

This brings me to a situation that I remember quite well. One lunchtime, working quite hard, the Chef appeared at the entrance to cold fish. He said, "Michael, there have been a few changes." It was very rare for the Chef himself to come and tell me things like this directly, but he had thought of it as he walked past from the larder.

"I see that you're using a tomato coulis on your terrine d'homard Romilly?"

"Yes Chef, the tomato coulis that you suggest we always use."

"Oh, there might be a small problem. Mr Colenso is using a strawberry sauce for his dessert. We can't have two red sauces on the menu. Go and tell Mr Colenso that he will need to change the sauce," he said, passing the buck to me.

Mr Colenso was the pastry chef – the head of pastry. He was the South African with a George Michael beard that I had met on my first day. He was an amazing patisserie chef, but everyone feared him. Probably because he was always quiet as if he was in deep thought.

"Me, Chef?" I asked.

"Of course, you, I wouldn't have said so otherwise…"

"OK Chef," I replied, and he walked away.

I stood there for a moment and paused – and thought, why me? Why have I got to go to Mr Colenso? No one ever called him 'chef'. They called him Mr Colenso because he preferred that. I tried to avoid going to the pastry kitchen. The only time I would go there was when we were making terrines – where we'd spend five minutes mixing it in the Hobart machine and then 30 minutes making it spotless – or when we had to create an en croûte with pastry.

On this occasion, I took a deep breath and asked the lads to hold the fort. I walked down through the busy kitchen into the basement where the pastry was located. When you got down to the pastry it was a totally different atmosphere. In the main kitchen, there was hustle and bustle, shouting and pots and pans clattering, machines making noise, waiters running left to right. The pastry was still. The chefs there were working with not a word coming out of their mouths, as they assembled amazing creations.

Mr Colenso had a box-shaped office in the centre of his kitchen with windows right round it so he could see every single one of his staff and the operation. There wasn't room to swing a cat in there – in fact there wasn't even room for a stool – so he had this upright desk that was built in just above his waist and he would lean forward on it writing away while occasionally looking through the windows. I think he was basically planning all the things the pastry needed to do. As I approached, I took another deep breath and looked across and saw a couple of my friends who I'd have lunch with, and they nodded at me. The sous chef gave me a steady, stern look as I approached Mr Colenso.

I walked in, and knocked on the window. It took a couple of seconds and then Mr Colenso looked up – and he mumbled. You had to really peel your ears back to understand what he was saying. His words to me (with a very thick South African accent) were, "What do *you* want?"

I apologised and said, "Excuse me Mr Colenso, the Chef has sent me down."

"What does the Chef want?"

"He's instructed me to tell you you'll have to change the sauce for the lunchtime party." I was hoping he wasn't going to look at the clock because it was already 12.15pm and the party was sitting down at 1pm.

"What do you mean I will have to change *my* sauce?"

"Well, what's happened is we're using the tomato sauce to go with the terrine de Romilly as the starter and you have a strawberry sauce to go with your terrine at the end." In fact, I think it was an ice cream bombe – made from meringue, filled with fruits and with a sponge base at the bottom of it. It wasn't for me to say the Chef hadn't thought it through properly, but I could thoroughly understand that with such a busy hotel, it could slip.

He looked at me and said, "So is the Chef telling me I have to change my sauce?" and I said "Yes". I looked to my left and saw the strawberries he was looking at. "Well, bloody hell. The Chef doesn't know whether he wants a shit or a haircut today, what is going on upstairs?" was his reply.

I said, "It's just busy." "And so are we," he replied. He looked to the side and saw a pile of mangoes.

"Well, you'd better roll your sleeves up and start peeling those mangoes; we'll use them for the sauce." With that he called Ian Coleman, his sous chef, and instructed him that this mango sauce had to be ready for the dessert for the 1pm sit down. Ian looked at me in utter horror and said, "Is it true?" I said yes. "So why are you down here telling me?"

"Because Chef instructed me to."

"My god man, you smell of fish," he said to me. I did want to reply that I worked on the fish section, but I thought enough damage had been done.

I thought I'd done my bit but as I turned to walk away Mr Colenso said to me, "Where are you going?"

"I'm going back upstairs," I replied.

"No, no no, no you can start prepping those mangoes, you got us into this shit!"

I said to myself, got you into what shit? But out loud, I said "Yes Chef, of course" instead, despite knowing that I had my own team to manage and wondering how I was going to get the message to them that I was now stuck in the pastry, having to prepare mangoes. It was very silent in there; no one was speaking to anyone else, and I couldn't find the right way to pluck up the courage to tell Mr Colenso that I needed to get back upstairs. But luckily, I was about to be rescued albeit in a very abrupt way.

I carried on and the Chef appeared at the door. "Oh Mr Colenso, did this young man tell you what was going on?"

"I know and we're getting on with it," he replied.

"But Michael, what are you still doing down here?"

"Well, I'm prepping the mango," I responded.

"So, you want to work in the pastry now?" he retorted.

I didn't know how to answer and said, "Not really today Chef, one day maybe, but not today."

"Oh well, I don't know why you're hanging around down here preparing mangoes when your section is really busy upstairs."

Thoroughly annoyed, I said, "Yes Chef", but was also very happy he had relieved me. Ian gave me an exasperated look as I left and rushed back up the stairs, taking a big sigh of relief that I could return to my work.

I got back to the main kitchen and rushed through to the fish section. The busy lunch service didn't finish until around 2 o'clock. In a big hotel, work is never finished. Once you get one service out of the way, you start preparing for the next. And bearing in mind we were working in London's best hotel, everything was prepared fresh.

Later that afternoon, after we had got the lunchtime party out of the way, I was about to send the lads on a quick five-minute break to gather their thoughts, before we plunged back into the afternoon. But it wasn't to be.

Suddenly over the intercom the Chef was calling everyone. "Everybody, get to the front now!" As I followed the instruction, I could see some commotion around the rotisserie department and the Chef was letting rip at the chef de partie on there.

"They're all wrong, they're not going to work, STOP STOP STOP everybody! I want everybody over here." It was all hands on deck.

"I want you all to prep. I need all these pommes soufflées ready for the party."

A pomme soufflée is a potato that is cut very thin but against the grain and across the grain. So, once it hits the hot fat it will perforate like a pillow, and three or four were served per portion. A crazy thing to do for a banqueting party, but who was I to judge the Chef. As most sections had fryers or fritters, as they were called, for shallow frying food, they asked everyone to help.

Every section in the kitchen was totally frustrated with what was going on and had to stop their busy afternoons to prepare the potatoes. We managed to carry this out – it's amazing how many light hands make quick work. For a party of over 200 covers we quickly had the pommes soufflées ready. And as they tested them, the first few worked, and the Chef dismissed us, allowing the chef de partie to finish the job.

We all went back to our sections, now about an hour behind, and we could all feel the stress of the day. It felt like one minute we were ahead and the next an hour behind. The sous chefs didn't care; they just harassed you more and wondered why you were struggling. You couldn't give them an excuse, so you just basically pressed on whilst they were in your ears like drill instructors.

There were a few exceptions. Dave Sharland was one of the sous chefs and was probably one of the funniest guys in the kitchen. He'd been at The Savoy a long time and had started there as a young lad and worked his way through the ranks. He was well liked by everyone, and he was always helping people. He didn't just bark the orders and walk off. He would always come and help if you were really 'in it'. Or he would explain things to you if you hadn't done them before. I found he was a great asset to ask if you were ever stuck.

Dave came up to me and he said, "How are you getting on? Are you alright? You've got enough of everything ready for tonight?" After I replied yes, he responded, "I'll just have a look round with you" and with his clipboard he went through the fridge with me and gave me a pat on the shoulder. "Well prepped. If you have five minutes, could you give the guys on veg a couple of your guys to help out?" I made sure that my guys had enough of their own to do. I hated this. I didn't want my team depleted again. I always wanted to get ahead.

It came to that evening, and we had seven parties going on, some in large banqueting and some in private rooms, and a couple of small parties which were very important alongside a gala dinner in the restaurant. The service was like an orchestra; everything was being called out and every chef – in harmony – would scream back "Yes Chef!" for the whole evening.

I could hear all of the instructions coming through my intercom. I was listening out for Aubrey or John, my cousins on the hot fish section. As soon as I heard them scream if they were getting short of a certain item, I would be ahead of them and be getting them out of the fridge and meeting them halfway to their section. This was alongside preparing the cold dishes coming out of the kitchen.

I tried to work very fast and in unison because if we were out of time with hot fish then you could be in hot water. The chef de partie on that section was Ian Moore, my namesake, though he was nothing like me. Blonde, slim, he always had a frown on his face, and walked with a ladle in his hands, swinging it. He was always going mad and would hit people with it. Noel, who started the same day as me, worked on hot fish and was the whipping boy for the first few weeks on there. I felt sorry for him and wanted to go up to Ian on many occasions and say stop picking on him, but it wouldn't be a wise thing to do – Ian was a guy who took no prisoners. It wasn't unusual for him to run through the kitchen f-ing and blinding at everyone. Although he shared pleasantries when we had everything ready, there were other times when he would tell me that my guys were shit and have it out with me in the locker room.

That day, though, was a horrendous day; it was really busy. Although in reality it was no longer than the others, it felt like the longest day, which is why it stuck in my mind. But for all the trials and tribulations that happened that day it was also a fantastic day – this is the reason I was happy to be a Savoy Boy.

INGREDIENTS FOR SUCCESS

Working long days made me a stronger person. It also made me very tired, but it brought out the reserves in me; it made me believe that I could achieve many things in a day. At the time I thought it was relentless and wondered when it was going to end. But then your body adapts, your mind adapts, and you find a way to achieve the long days.

It was like a brain exercise most of the time; you're young, you're physical, you can do it, but your mind had to do it every time to keep moving on. I realised working eight hours is very easy for me. I could achieve a lot more than most chefs in a day and I solved problems a lot quicker. Sometimes unexpected things go wrong in a hotel, but the great thing is that my mind was always prepared for the shortage of staff or the late arrival of goods to cook with, so I was always ahead of the game.

Working the occasional long day always helped me and it's built into my system now because I always work until the job is done. When you're working with a team that thinks the same way, it's the only way you're going to achieve more and more.

Fiona Tanzi Costa serving apprenticeship with pastry chef Peter Webb

Jason and Matthew

Cold fish under siege - Michael, Dave Sharland, Matthew, Brian and two others

Laurence Robinson

The stove used by Escoffier and still in service in the mid '70s

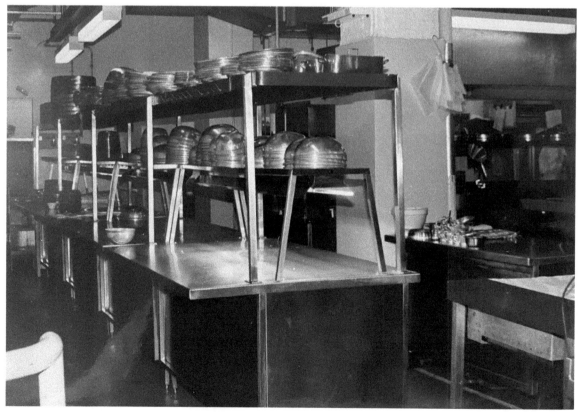

A temporary kitchen arrangement

Achievement of more awards

The corridor through the kitchen during the building works. A waiter makes his way to the restaurant

Michael (second left) and Alan Maw (centre) with others

Hildred and Duncan Weekes

Dave Sharland

After a busy service what are you
doing on the phone. Michael?

Everything has to be weighed before accepting

Mr Luigi, maître d'

The new brigade for the new kitchen. 1985. 75% of the chefs turned up for the photo.

Chef standing with proud members of his brigade

Sous chef presentation

The pass in the new kitchen

David and Simon can't resist a pose between service

Even though busy, in between service and prep time would bring out the
good side of most chefs David and Anne having a moment.

Gordon, chef de partie, plating up with
Laurence (sous chef). I'd never seen Gordon
smile so they must have been sharing a joke.

Hard-working Papa Ali organised all the other
kitchen porters while keeping busy himself

These guys, the kitchen porters, were the
backbone of the kitchen. We called them
all Ali but this wasn't a lack of respect
as without them nothing flowed. We had
lots of banter with these great chaps.

To cook and look the part was all about
being a professional and Aubrey Williams
is keeping the standards high here.

Chef de partie Sue on potage. There weren't many girls in the hot kitchens but the few that there were worked just as hard or harder than the lads. Sue held her own and was well respected.

Julian Marshall and me on veg section after service. Jules was always moving at 100 miles an hour. 'Push, push' is what he always said.

Gordon, Simon, Phil, Ian and Peter posing on the sauce section for a memorable picture

The quiet man John Wood being caught
out by the flash of Aubrey's camera.
Hot fish was a busy section

Eddie the head carver

Grand dining

Dominique Happart (centre) and Graeme Watson (right) with Dominique's first prize
menu awards in the Mouton Rothschild Back of House Skills Competition

Meanwhile back on cold fish, here I
am stopping for a quick shot

Peter Webb looking happy and proud in
front of his masterpiece wedding cake

The old kitchen was very hot and the coal oven was coming to a sad end. Chef
had a vision to turn everything around and what a great job he did.

Willie Bauer - the human side

Mid-service in the new kitchen, busy but smiling faces. It was an easy life on hot fish.

The old kitchen: my good mate Lindon prepares the steak and kidney pies for service

Dorothy, Duncan, Julian, Gordo, Vito, Garry, Laurence - a late-night pose. It must have been a good service with such smiles all round.

Teamwork at its best with maitre d' Mr Luigi winning a second rosette - hard work always pays off

Busy prepping salmon

*After a busy service boys and girls often let off steam. A normal evening
with picture taken by yours truly on Aubrey's camera.*

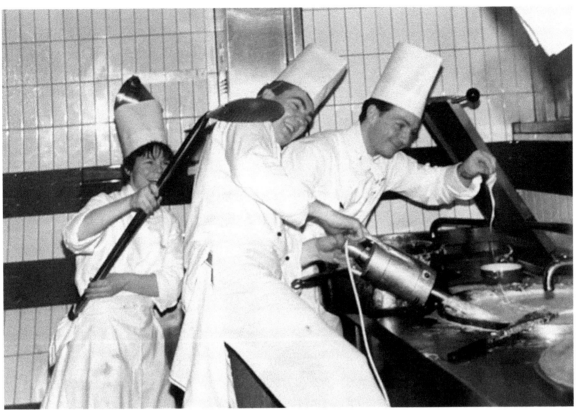

Sue, David and Simon

Michael with Noel who looks as if he is off to a rodeo

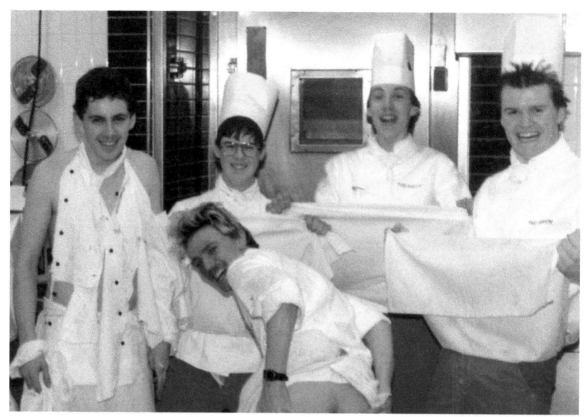

Camaraderie important at work and play

Chef with the sous chefs

Soft lads

Dave Sharland, Ian Moore and Chef discussing a dish

Congratulations on a job well done Chef and maître d Mr Luigi

Different era with one familiar face Julian Jenkins looks straight at the camera

David and Simon

Hildred working hard at the fat fryers

Brian Whiting (left) making afternoon tea sandwiches in the larder section

Bossie and Vito

The team of waiters who make the complete picture for service

Bossie admiring his work in the cold kitchen at night

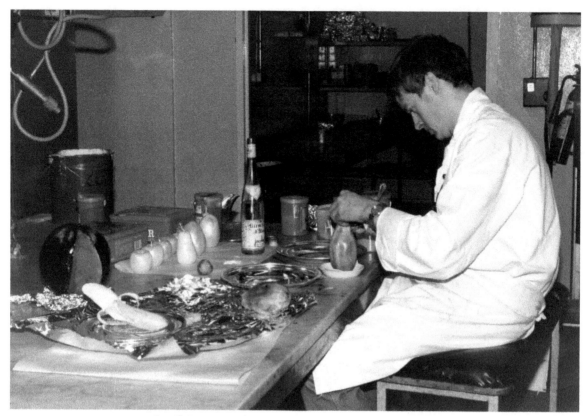

Ian Coleman in the pastry department pulling sugar

Dave Sharland up to no good behind the cloches

Bossie at work

Wayne Bosworth outside the Lincoln Room

Back (left to right): Adam, Charlotte and
Ben. At front John and John

CHAPTER 10:
KEEPING IT REAL

I was early Thursday morning, and I'd just arrived. I was down in the locker room, situated in the basement. You had to walk up these narrow twirly steps and then you'd reach a winding corridor that took you upwards towards the kitchen.

As you approached the kitchen, you could smell the food, the stocks being made, bones being roasted, and different smells would approach your nose. Alongside the smells, you could hear noise and feel intense heat. And you could tell how busy the kitchen was before you even reached the doors.

On that day, not only was there heat, but I could also hear a lot of noise. More than normal. What was going on? It was 6.15 in the morning.

I entered the kitchen and saw that Arthur, the breakfast chef, who was usually calm and getting his orders out, was rushing around and there was a lot of commotion. Normally I would just swing a sharp right and walk through the larder and the butchery, straight to the cold fish section, but that day my curiosity got the better of me.

As I walked towards where Arthur was working, the restaurant manager screamed at me. "Quickly quickly, help out here. We need two poached eggs; we need eggs Benedict. Hurry up, hurry up."

With my knives still under my arms, I realised Arthur was totally snowed under with orders. Dropping my knives where I was, I looked across. "Arthur, how can I help?"

Arthur was in his fifties, and mumbled in his Spanish accent. I couldn't understand a word he was saying. In all my time at The Savoy, I struggled to understand what he said.

I looked at the checks (the terminology for the orders) and said to him, "Tell me what you need, I'll get it ready, and you plate it."

"Si, si, si, si," he replied as the other chefs arrived and we realised we were in a world of hell.

We just cracked on with helping Arthur out as best we could – it was a good part of an hour we were at it. It was like a midday service, but with one man. Around a quarter to eight, the first rush was over, and Arthur had it under control by then.

"What happened there?" I asked. The other chefs agreed; it was bloody crazy.

Arthur replied, "I can't do this; this is too much, it's too much."

You would have thought that Arthur was born just to be the breakfast chef. He was a short man, with what you would you call a customary Spanish moustache. Not long afterwards, later that morning, when he was clearing down, I approached him. "My god, you got hit this morning."

In his broken English he replied, "Yeah, nobody told me that they had a breakfast function." At The Savoy we had a function for everything – breakfast functions, lunchtime functions, afternoon tea functions – and it never seemed to stop. Unfortunately, poor Arthur had been caught out.

He started telling me about his life as I continued to help him. It was a very quiet morning for me, so I spent time helping him out.

He said, "Oh you know when I was a younger man, I was just like you."

"Really, Arthur?" I replied.

He said, "Yes I was not always doing breakfast – I was a head chef, a really good head chef."

I smirked a little, which was rude of me, saying, "Really?"

He said, "Yes, why don't you believe me? I tell you, years ago I worked as a head chef." I listened and entertained his conversation, thinking nothing more of it. And then 10 minutes later, as I returned to my cold fish section, Arthur walked through as he was going home. "Michael!"

"Yes Arthur."

He said, "Look at this", and took some clippings out of a tatty folded envelope that he had under his arm. "This is me." And there was the younger version of Arthur, and he was working as a head chef in Madrid and the title stated that they had just achieved honours at the hotel under Executive Chef Arthur. I stood back in amazement. "I was a very good head chef, but when you get older and older, you know you can't stand behind the stoves, you mustn't stand behind the stoves. You'll end up like me. I do breakfast now because I'm not good enough to do anything else."

I said, "I'm sure you've still got that in your closet."

"No, no, no no, those days are gone now. I want an easy life, so I decided to do the breakfast. When I first came here to The Savoy I did more than the breakfast, but as you get older, you know the old bones can't handle it anymore."

I wondered why he had decided to stay on at The Savoy and do the breakfast. Why did he not do what most chefs do? You do your time, working in the kitchen until you get to around 45. Then you start thinking that you can't be standing behind a hot stove when you're 50. That was my goal anyway; I decided early on that I didn't want to do that. It's not good for you or your body.

But Arthur loved being in the kitchen so much and didn't want to leave. In a way he normally had an easy life; he could work Monday to Friday and know that other chefs would cover a weekend. I presume in those days there weren't any other options for chefs like there are today. Most chefs end up being food and beverage directors, or they go and work for other industries involving food, but not so intense.

In a way being a chef at your highest level is like being a professional footballer or sportsman. There is a period when you're on your way up and you fight like crazy to get up to your peak. Then you have a certain number of years that you're at your peak, maybe a good decade, depending upon your stamina. Then you find that someone else behind you has a new idea or the place where you're working is changing their way of thinking, and your ideas are out of date, so you move on. After you've passed your peak, it's time to go and do something else.

This had happened to Arthur. When he faced his reality and realised that he was on his way down, he looked for something else that he would enjoy.

And if you love food as much as I do and as I'm sure most of the chefs I've worked with do, they go on to things like opening up restaurants and having younger guys run them for them under their guidance, or if they do quit the industry, they find something else that's not so strenuous and become home cooks, keeping the hobby of loving food in their home kitchens whilst they carry out their new jobs.

It's fortunate that some of us, in this modern day, end up doing things that continue to involve us in food. I, for one, would never quit this industry; I love it too much. For me it isn't just about the food, it's about the fantasy, it's about the whole experience of looking at how the farmers are producing something for us chefs to produce something for our customers to consume. The whole chain of it excites me. I wouldn't say I'm past my peak because my peak is still in my head, but I do look at food and the way it works these days in a different light.

All those years I was at The Savoy, all I wanted to do was work to the best of my ability. I think I have achieved that, and more. I still have branded in my head that "if you can work at The Savoy, you can work anywhere". I didn't understand it while I was there, but it helped me on many occasions to get jobs once I had left The Savoy. Working there enabled me to experience so much – new dishes, flavours and approaches – and make friends who I have kept in touch with and am proud of, and when we meet we share old stories. And the funny thing about it is the glimpse I get of The Savoy in their style of work when I go to visit their restaurants. This is how things grow.

INGREDIENTS FOR SUCCESS

———————————

To be confident and believe in yourself are things that grow with time. Being arrogant and obnoxious can be your downfall. In many walks of life there are people who learn quickly and people that take a little bit longer. To be a good person is to always be there for the people who are not so quick to catch on. Be available to help. I always kept myself real, and I never had to go around shouting how good I was because that was inside me.

So, if you see a fellow man or woman in need of your help, being there to support them is more than anyone could ask. This is all part of teamwork and if you only believe in yourself and don't believe in others, you're not really keeping it real.

CHAPTER 11:
BEING BLACK

One of the things about working in such a prestige establishment in the 1980s was that there weren't many people of colour. In fact, in a brigade of over 100 people, there must have only been two or three of us of ethnic origin in the kitchen. We had to work twice as hard to be noticed – although I wasn't going to allow anything to stop me from getting from where I wanted to get to. Colour, creed, nationality – I was born British and am very proud of it. But unfortunately, even in places like The Savoy, you would occasionally hit a wall. Most of those walls came when you were looking for promotion or recognition.

In my first year I'd worked so hard, alongside other lads who had started at the same time. Aubrey Williams started a month after me. We struck up a friendship from day one. We got on well and he had the same understanding of success and what we wanted – and we worked hard. He was one of my best friends back then, and still is today.

A year after he started at The Savoy, Aubrey got promoted to chef de partie – I was so pleased for him – alongside my friend John. They were both promoted in the same week, and I wondered why I hadn't been. How come they had got promoted and I'd been working as first commis on the cold fish section and hadn't been considered? I had worked hard, and I actually felt that I had worked even harder, and by then Simon had left cold fish, and I had more responsibility in the section.

I was patiently waiting for the moment when the Chef would come and whisper in my ear, "Mr Moore, you've worked hard, I want to promote you." But it never happened. So in the end I decided to speak with him.

One afternoon, after lunchtime service, I summoned up my bravery and knocked on the door of his office. As I knocked on his door, he said "Come in" in his perfect but accented English. "Michael, what do you want, what can I do for you?"

"Chef, can I have a word?"

"Is it important?" he replied.

"Yes Chef."

"Oh well come in."

I walked into the office and stood there; he was writing something. He asked me to sit down, so I did nervously, seeing how busy he was with so many things. His secretary came in and added some papers to his table. I sat there patiently for a few moments.

"Go on, fire away."

"Well Chef..." I said hesitantly.

"Get it off your chest, what are you mumbling about?" he responded.

"Well Chef I was wondering, I've been working on the cold fish for a year now..."

Before I could finish my sentence, he said, "Oh you want to change?"

"No, I'm quite happy there, Chef."

"So, what's the problem then?"

I said, "There's no problem at all."

"So, I don't know what you're doing here then." I felt like he was starting to dismiss me.

"Well Chef to be perfectly honest I just want to know – I would like to be promoted, because I ..."

He didn't let me finish my sentence. "Promoted?!"

"Yes, I'm working as first commis."

"I know that."

"I'd like my position to change to chef de partie because I run the section anyway since Simon has left and I was wondering..."

"Well, you know it's a lot of responsibility as chef de partie, Michael," he reminded me.

"Yes Chef, but I do all of that responsibility for the last few months now – it's just been me and the four other lads and I have to arrange and write the rotas."

"Oh, I didn't know that, the sous chefs never told me."

I said, "Well erm, basically it's me Chef running the cold fish."

He said, "I'll think about it. You know it's a lot of pressure."

I felt as if he hadn't heard a word I'd just said, so I left the office, not completing my argument with him, not wanting to annoy him. I went back to the cold fish and felt deflated. I did my job as well as the other guys; we had to work in tandem. If they were pleased with what I was doing, what was the problem?

It wasn't about money, as the promotion would only result in a few pounds more per week, but it was status that was important for me and my CV and future career.

In reality, Anton Edelmann was managing a team of over 100 chefs. It was incredibly busy and as long as the job was getting done, the Chef wouldn't think about promotions. But we wanted to be respected, and rather than take action, we'd often whinge to one of the sous chefs about the unfairness of it all.

Later that day, Dave Sharland, one of my favourite sous chefs, came on the late shift. He saw me looking dejected. "What's going on Bimbo?" he asked, using my nickname that Stuart McLeod, one of the first commis, had bestowed on me. Although it was said with a joke and affection.

"Nothing," I replied, although he wasn't convinced.

He said, "This isn't like you. You're normally really sparky and funny."

I said, "Yeah yeah, I spoke with Chef today. I asked him if I could be promoted, Dave."

"And? What did he say?"

"He didn't say no but he didn't say yes." I then went on, "I don't get it Dave; I mean is my work bad?"

"Course it isn't."

"So, I can't understand it."

"You've got to understand... The Chef doesn't see everything that goes on, he just sees the completed work and that's what you've got to convince him."

"Yeah, well Simon left two months ago and it's like nothing's changed – it's still the same standards."

"I tell you what, when he comes through to see you in the section and he's here, ask him again."

"Ok, great idea," I responded.

With that he went on his way. A few days went by, and I tried to pluck up courage again.

It was a Friday morning. I remember it well because it was hell day – the first double bill day of the week. Every day was busy, but Fridays and Saturdays had the distinctive mark that you were going to 'be in the shit'. At around 10am, the Chef came running through.

"Oh, Michael have you got the terrines done for tonight? I want a sample in my office in 10 minutes?"

"Yes Chef," I responded.

Then he went out to the larder, and he said similar things to the larder chef about things he needed done. And then he popped back to me and asked to see the timbales. We used to make these special timbales with the finest mousse. We'd pass the fish through a sieve three or four times and then it was gently made with the cream and egg whites and the fish. We then added beluga caviar in the middle and steamed them very gently. It was a very delicate dish.

"I'm doing them right now, Chef."

He watched me for a while and said, "Good and make sure you pass it through two more times." He dipped his finger in and tried it.

I said, "Chef, do you remember what I was speaking to you about the other day in your office about being promoted?"

With that he looked at me and said, "I've already done it, don't let me down" and he walked off. I carried on working for a few moments thinking done what? Already done what? I didn't understand.

That day was like a storm. Busy and tiring. Remember I was still only 21, but I was suffering from backache. It was so intense; it seemed relentless. At around 11 o'clock that night, as service was calming down and we were all cleaning down the section, Dave Sharland came back through and gave me one hell of a slap on the back. "I told you, I told you, the old man said you're the new chef de partie of cold fish."

"Oh, is that what he was telling me earlier?" Now it made sense. I'd been promoted. A strange way to do it, but I didn't care. I was now a chef de partie.

I was so excited and so happy and on Saturday morning I was in work even earlier just to announce I was chef de partie and to get it in writing! I don't think any of the other lads took any notice, reminding me that they thought I was doing the job already, because I had effectively been doing so for the last few months.

It was a proud moment, because when I arrived at The Savoy, I was only a commis, just like a workhorse, and to achieve this promotion in just over a year made me feel proud inside. But in the back of my mind, I wondered if he was unsure about me doing the job. Was it because I was a black guy?

In a way there was a bit of truth about it all, I think, when you have to trust someone of colour and you've never had to put yourself in that position before, and for him it must have been different. Coming from Germany, working in Britain, first of all the British chefs weren't the favourite nation in the kitchen, but they proved themselves to get promoted. And then came along this black guy who was British. And to promote him was another decision he had to make.

But I will always be grateful to him for making that decision because for me it broke down barriers. It made me believe that I could tell other black boys and girls that they could do what I was doing. In a way I think I was a little bit naïve because it didn't really get any easier. It seemed that everywhere I went I would always have this barrier.

INGREDIENTS FOR SUCCESS

The most shocking thing for me was finding out that I was at a disadvantage being black. It's just a colour but to others it can mean a lot more. I don't walk around every day thinking I'm black, but I do work as hard as the next man to achieve. Some people found this a threat and would use my colour to put me in a disadvantaged position and from the time I went to college to become a chef I realised I would have to work twice as hard to achieve the same goal as my white colleagues.

This didn't put me off as it was something that my parents drummed into me. My mother would always say, "Whatever you do, Michael, you will be in the spotlight because of your colour. Just make it count to your advantage and take their negativity and turn it into positive."

What I can say I learnt at The Savoy is that if you were good at what you did in the kitchens, they didn't see colour. I can say that honestly back in the mid-80s there was a lot of racial tension, but I didn't experience very much of it in The Savoy, and on the few occasions I did, it was dealt with very bluntly.

If you are a person of colour, remember this, you are unique, and this is the only weapon that a negative person will have against you. Keep on going forward, share your worth and stay ahead.

CHAPTER 12:
THE OLD MAN

Looking back, it was funny how we called Anton Edelmann the 'old man', because he was only around 36 years old when I joined The Savoy. But remember that most of us lads were in our late teens and early 20s, so it felt like he was much older than us.

He left south Germany to work at The Savoy when he was a young man. He started working there when he was 18 and stayed there for a year before he left and went to work around London. He worked in various different establishments before he came back to The Savoy as Executive Chef. I think that alone is an achievement, to come back to the hotel where you started.

In my conversations with the Chef over the last few months he told me that when he took over that job the hotel was in a different place. He thought he had bitten off more than he could chew. He told me it was great that he had a strong team around him that helped him a lot. If only he had used those words back then, I think a lot of the lads would have understood him much better. They all worked hard for him because they respected him but sometimes, he would stand there in the wilderness while we worked so many hours thinking the Chef didn't care. I think he always cared but when you're the boss you have to show leadership; there can't be any cracks in your armour.

The Chef reported to Willie Bauer who was the director of the hotel. Another strong German, he was a perfectionist who liked everything to be structured and just so. He was a tough director. He didn't mince his words because he wanted to turn The Savoy Hotel around and make it unique.

As the Chef told me, when he and Willie arrived at the hotel, it was on its knees. Long before I arrived, they had to sell off a section of the hotel and make it into private apartments because they were close to bankruptcy.

Anton Edelmann (Chef), Willie Bauer (general manager), John Wood (chef de partie) and Barry Colenso (pastry chef) at Independence Day celebrations

Willie knew that with a strong and modern kitchen, the hotel would go places. He also knew that Anton Edelmann was the right person to lead it. They had a vision of where they wanted the hotel to be, and they made it work.

Within two years the hotel had been turned around and was winning awards. Suddenly The Savoy Hotel that had been sitting dormant was coming alive again. The prestige of the hotel was back.

On a Saturday the Chef would normally arrive around six or seven in the evening, perhaps a little earlier. He would suddenly appear like he had been there all day. You would hear his distinctive warm voice as, like many with a south German accent, he rolled his Rs.

He would do this thing where he'd come up to you and embrace you with his arm underneath your shoulder and he would say, "You know Michael, there are two types of chefs in this world. In fact, let me rephrase that. There are two types of cooks in this world. There's the cook who chucks it all together and hopes for the best and then there's the other one who takes time and control and recognises that he's working with a precious object and produces perfection on a plate."

And then he'd squeeze your shoulder and go, "Which one are you?" and of course you would say you were the latter! "Oh well, let's hope so. Are you ready for tonight?" he'd say. And of course, you'd answer, "Yes Chef!" There was no other word to call him. It was very rare that you would hear anyone call him by his name. I think I only ever heard him being called by his name once in my presence and that was by the maître d', Mr Luigi. Most of the time everyone in the hotel, from the personnel to the guests, addressed him as 'Chef'.

It was a thing of honour and respect being called 'Chef'; it meant that you were number one, and at The Savoy we knew that. We were cooks until we were called a chef. Despite all the titles like chef de partie and first commis and chef tournant and pastry chef, we all knew that there was only one Chef and that was Anton Edelmann.

I always found the Chef to be fair, despite some of our interactions during the time I worked under him at The Savoy, and had a very good relationship with him. I would like to think that he got on well with me. But he knew that I was ambitious, and he also knew that I could be very moody, and he would use that to his advantage on many occasions.

He knew how to get the most out of the chefs. When he felt that his kitchen wasn't working well, there were certain chefs whose skin he knew he could get under and their temperament, or their moodiness, would bring it all back into gear. We weren't the type of people to shout blame. We knew that if the Chef was having a go at us he had respect for us and he wanted us to do well and I know that because I've witnessed it many a time at The Savoy. When the Chef had no more interest in you, he wouldn't even say "Morning" to you – he would just walk past and I think that was even more hurtful than being told off, giving you a royal kick up the arse. If you didn't get it right first time, he'd lose it. But this always served to make you do better than you thought you could ever do.

Working with these types of people, you realised that Germans have a work ethic that makes a lot of countries look very ordinary. They would say to their kids, whatever job they wanted to do, they had to be the best. This was the ethic running through the hotel. You could feel it through the management team; everybody had to give an extra pound of flesh to be there. You weren't just there to do a job, you were there on merit, you were there to move the hotel to go forward.

INGREDIENTS FOR SUCCESS

With his knowledge, how he held himself and his beard, it did feel like Anton Edelmann was a lot older than he was. As young chefs, we'd idolised the Chef, and I wanted to be like him. To be 36 and running a kitchen that big and making decisions on his feet when things went wrong, without knowing what the outcome would be, was incredible. I learnt patience, discipline and control.

I don't think Chef minded the name at all; I'm sure he must have heard it being whispered on many occasions. As long as we weren't calling him it to his face, he just let it pass, so I salute the name 'old man' as I think it is an honour to be held in high esteem and respected. So, think about who you hold in high esteem and respect them.

CHAPTER 13:
TIMING AND
TEAMWORK

S aturday mornings had a calm and relaxed air about them. We would arrive
around 7am and regardless of how busy we were, they always seemed to be fun.

It's likely that your sections would have been through the most horrendous
week, and you wanted to get ready for the big push on Saturday. We would often have
a gala dinner and dance alongside à la carte meals, so needed to have enough prep to
cover the likely numbers.

Most chefs de partie would do their utmost best to get the weekends off, but that
never really happened, especially as you were the chief of the department, reporting
to the sous chef. It was also likely that the sous chefs wouldn't arrive until midday and
the old man didn't come in until much later.

So it was left to the chefs de partie to just get things done. We all knew what we had
to do but we did it at a slower pace. You would have time to walk in and say good
morning, have a coffee, and chat with the other chefs.

What made it feel different was people like Brian Whiting and Wayne Bosworth,
making their little jokes around the kitchen. Mark 'Biggins' Fletcher was one of the
main characters (sauce), and he and Stuart McLeod (veg), a big strapping Bristol boy,
would be in there making their jokes, making everyone laugh. They'd be giving us
'shit' in a calm way, about things that we didn't do right during the week. Chefs de
partie would mingle and chat away, but also keep one eye on what their subordinates
were doing.

On Saturday mornings, Brian would often be up to no good. When the Chef wasn't in
his office, if his beloved Liverpool was playing, he would bring up his radio from his

locker and you would suddenly hear the commentary blasting through the intercom. Or you'd see him messing around on the microphone – calling out false orders or imitating the old man or other chefs.

This brought us back down to earth and made us realise that we were human beings and out of all the stress of the whole week we would still find time to be real. I think that's how I got to know a lot of the lads while I was there. Not just because of their strengths and how they wanted to be and where they wanted to go with their careers, but I also got to learn their characters and understand who they were as individuals.

As the evening service grew, the sous chefs would be in control of the pass. The sous chef would stand on the other side of the pass to you, and you would present the food and the sauce in front of them. They would complete the plate and then it would be sent into the restaurant. The saucier and the poissonier, and the rôtisseur and the entremetier had to be in sync.

When you were working on the cold section some of your starters would be going out with the hot food. The great thing about that was that the cold starters could be prepared just a few minutes before the hot food was finished. If you had a combination dish, where it was a cold starter with heated elements to it, the waiters would pick up the plate from the back and take it to the front. The poissonier would place his element of warm food on that plate and it would be sent. It was all about precision and timing.

Timing is everything to a successful kitchen – and teamwork. And these were very important to all of us. We all hated it when someone was lagging or wasn't ready and that's what made the kitchen work. I've worked in many kitchens in my life and I've run many kitchens but I must say The Savoy was like a well-oiled machine for the size of the brigade.

As times move on and everything evolves, kitchens change; there is less labour, more machinery takes over, and food is brought in pre-prepared. So you lose that element of total manpower and trust. You're having to trust stuff that's already been pre-prepared in a lot of kitchens. I love the fact that I can prepare something from 'zero to hero' as we would call it. This was another of my favourite sayings from Wayne Bosworth; he would love to do things from nothing to something and he would admire it. I think we all felt satisfied when we did something well.

When you're in the middle of a busy service and there's screaming and things going on, from the outside it looks like total stress. But once we got into a groove in that kitchen, we could serve all night. It gave us all a buzz because by the time end of service came, we were literally looking at one another, bright red faces, sweat running down our foreheads, war wounds of slightly burned or cut fingers BUT we'd achieved an amazing service that evening. And to think we would have the opportunity to do it all again – madness! If you're a chef, you'll totally understand what I mean. The excitement of so many talented people working as one and producing such great food.

Sundays were mostly a day of cleaning down and getting the kitchen ready for another busy week. Whatever staff you had left on the Sunday shift, you'd give them a list of stuff they needed to have ready for Monday morning. The people who worked on Sundays would still have to tolerate a busy Sunday lunch, but it was a set lunch, a selection of roasts served directly from a trolley. It was probably the easiest service of the week.

Mostly the tasks on a Sunday were mise en place, preparing what you needed for the coming week. So, by the time I would walk in on a Monday morning I could see the elements of what had been happening on a Sunday evening – if the team had been overrun with orders or if they had the time to get ready. And there was always a waiter I knew well to tattle tale if the Sunday night hadn't been busy and the boys had been standing around!

Monday could be a horrid day. You knew it was going to be the longest, longest day. Everything was coming at you, new orders, the Chef possibly not happy with things that had happened at the weekend. And even if he was happy with what had happened at the weekend, he would let you know about the few things that didn't go well. This was his way of keeping you on your toes for the next week.

****

Alongside the teamwork that had to happen to make the kitchen work smoothly, there would be silver trays floating around at head height in and out of the kitchen. Of course, these were attached to the waiters. Chefs and waiters – what a combination as they never saw eye to eye most of the time but complemented each other in the jobs that they did. There was often bickering if the tray wasn't straight, or the waiter was too noisy whilst waiting to pick up food. And I'm sure that the waiters had moans about the chefs – they took too long, the plates were too hot, they were always gabbling amongst themselves when they were busy in the restaurant. At times it felt like chaos, but we got the job done.

As much as I had my few run-ins with waiters, I never disrespected them. I understood that their job was just as unique as ours in its own way. The flamboyancy of a waiter could make your dish sound fabulous and the way it was presented would add 100+ points on top of what you'd already achieved. Watching a waiter carry away a plate that had just been decorated to perfection and seeing them ease through the swinging doors into the restaurant hoping they met their destination without any disaster was satisfying.

The waiter's uniform carried distinction and class. They wore cream jackets with a centre button with gold button tops and also on the epaulettes, which were paired with black trousers and uniform black shoes. It was a simple uniform but looked the part for such a prestigious hotel. And then there was the head waiter and restaurant manager, who would walk around in evening suits with tails. Distinguishing them from the straightforward waiter was easy; you could say they were the equivalent of the sous chef in the kitchen making sure that everything was leaving the kitchen at top notch, reaching its destination with perfection. Mr Luigi – the maitre d' – would appear on occasion in the kitchen, briefly chatting to the duty shift chefs or a head chef himself, making sure that service at both ends was going to work well.

I became very good friends with one of the waiters, Giuseppe, who would often pick up cold platters for starters from my section. We'd often have a joke, and I knew I could rely on him if I'd forgotten something and vice versa. We became good mates and used to chat in between service. Giuseppe would always make his jokes, telling me about small little incidents that happened inside the restaurant, things that made him chuckle, keeping me informed on what was going on, such as the restaurant being full so reminding me to keep on my toes or to let me know how service was going. It was good inside information to have as a chef, as once the swinging doors swung back you would not know what was going on behind them and he would always pass on compliments made by a particular table.

The fascinating thing about most of the waiters in the restaurant was that they already had connections; either a member of their families or close friends back in Italy had recommended them to The Savoy. A few of them were following in their father's footsteps as quite a few waiters' fathers had worked for the Savoy group which included great hotels like Claridge's, the Berkeley and the Connaught. All of these hotels and a few others were part of the Savoy group. Waiters and chefs would change from hotel to hotel after a couple of years and in those years the Savoy group was where most people wanted to be.

INGREDIENTS FOR SUCCESS

Working in The Savoy was totally all about team. We had our individual sections, but when you send in food from various sections, timing and teamwork is everything: a cold dish, a hot dish must arrive at their respective temperatures on the pass and only teamwork can achieve this.

Without teamwork, you don't have a kitchen. The same applies to any job and any situation where you want to achieve success.

CHAPTER 14:
SOMETHING DIFFERENT

Certain days of the week could be quite rewarding. One afternoon we were making the salmon and turbot en croûte. Fish wrapped in pastry to you! They were being made for a special function; it was one of those days when we weren't as busy as normal. It was the only large function we had on the whole day and the restaurant was only moderately busy. I prepared the en croûtes to be covered in pastry. There were 15 in number, and I placed them individually on the trolley and took them downstairs to the patisserie, to be wrapped by the guys in the pastry department.

There was a totally different atmosphere going on in pastry that day too. Mr Colenso wasn't in. Ian Coleman, the pastry sous chef, was in charge. I had a great relationship with Ian, and everyone seemed a lot more relaxed.

My friend Moses greeted me, approaching me with a big screaming hello and asking me what I had for them. I told them what help I needed, and the pastry boys agreed to wrap them in pastry and then cook them for me.

Moses took the trolley from me and wheeled it into the pastry department. Ian approached me and we had a chat for about 10 minutes. Then he asked me what was going on upstairs in the main kitchen and how I was feeling about my work. I found it very strange that he was asking me such questions, but I soon realised they were leading to something.

Then Anne, one of the girls who worked alongside Moses, looked at me and suggested that I could do well working pastry, but I'd never considered it. I'd always considered pastry chefs to be specialists. In fact, it is usually seen as a separate kitchen, outside of the main kitchen. But most great head chefs know about pastry, I thought to myself.

Ian told me that there were some vacancies coming up as a couple of the girls were leaving, and he asked me to give it some thought.

I went over to Moses, where he was with another chef, and he started to take the en croûtes off the trolley and wrap them in pastry. I watched as they expertly took my handiwork and made it into perfection. I realised that I would like to do that and then I was suddenly energised. So he invited me to try it and I wrapped the fish in pastry with his guidance. It came out well and Ian asked me to stay and help, which was a great offer as they didn't normally invite people to stay around and normally asked them to leave the food behind to be finished. As my section was covered, I stayed to help and continued to wrap the fish with pastry.

It was a very easy morning; everyone was talking, and it seemed surreal that we had time on our hands to get to know each other. When the pastry was completed, rather than wending my way back upstairs to use the ovens, the pastry guys put them in their brand-new confectionery ovens and started to bake them. In the meantime, I had a look round the pastry at the other things they were doing.

A couple of the girls were working on afternoon tea, making cakes in the glacier area: frangipane, strawberry tartes, chocolate boxes, petit fours. Small, beautiful cakes. All the sorbets were made there, as were the compotes and anything needed for the different sweet dishes. And as everything was made in house, there was one young chap who would make all of the different pastries – shortcut, puff, filo. In fact, any pastry needed, he would make it from scratch. The pastry department was also broken down into different roles, so they each knew exactly what they were doing.

It was another day when I explored this option a little further. I'd been drinking at the Coal Hole with some of my fellow chefs and I departed early, ready to go home and sleep before the next day. My mind was starting to race, and it was only about 9 or 10 o'clock in the evening. I said my goodnights and got jeered by the lads for leaving early. I walked up towards Covent Garden to grab the tube home to Turnpike Lane, which normally took about 20 to 25 minutes. As I arrived at Covent Garden station, I saw Ian a few strides ahead of me, so I called out his name and caught up with him. He was a softly spoken man and a little bit shy. He asked me where I was going, so I told him, and it turned out we were heading in the same direction.

As we jumped on the tube and found a seat, we carried on chatting where we left off about working in the pastry. I think he was trying to sell it to me in a big way, but I couldn't find the courage to tell him that it wasn't the right department for me. Still, I listened eagerly, eating up all the information about his department.

I suddenly popped out a question: "If Colenso left would you take over his job?" He looked at me, and said, "Do you know something I don't know?" Of course I didn't but I wanted to find out how long he planned to stay at The Savoy. He told me that he enjoyed the job and when he didn't enjoy it, it would be time to leave.

We got off the tube at Turnpike Lane and as we came up to the surface, we could smell dense smoke. We couldn't see a fire, but it was like something big was burning. Looking up the road, we saw fire engines racing away from us. And as we walked towards our homes, we could see fire in the distance. It was a dark night, but the sky was lit up with the smoke. It was the night of the Broadwater Farm riots in Tottenham and police cars, ambulances and fire engines raced past us nearly every second. It didn't look good. Ian turned right and bid me goodnight, and we went our separate ways.

Although I never did go into pastry at The Savoy, it made me think about my future and what might be ahead.

INGREDIENTS FOR SUCCESS

I was driven to learn everything. I worked in many departments in my whole career, and I did spend a few months working in pastry in one of the hotels, but if I could turn the clock back, The Savoy was probably one of the best places in the world to be if you wanted to learn to cook everything.

All the departments were well oiled, and I would recommend any young person to try something new as you never know where it may lead.

CHAPTER 15:
MIDNIGHT STARS

At the hotel we had a reputation for having many celebrity guests to stay. Although their names were kept under wraps even in the kitchen, they were given code names. This meant that there was a note of special requests for each of our special customers, which was kept on a board in the kitchen. So we knew who they were, their room number and how they liked their food prepared.

An order would come in and if the celebrity liked the way one of the chefs prepared that meal, then they would always be the chef that made that dish in the future. That's because you could give two chefs exactly the same ingredients and instructions together and they probably would both put it together extremely well, but The Savoy strived for consistency. And as celebrities can be superstitious, they would often eat the same thing.

Two of these code names were 'Blue Eyes' and 'Boots' and you may well have already guessed that this was code for Frank Sinatra and his daughter, Nancy. I made the first club sandwich for 'Blue Eyes' on the first day he stayed at the hotel, and he approved it. So, I ended up making it each day for the following 10 days. And it was always me who made it in the future, and likewise with his daughter's cheese and tomato sandwich.

Although we didn't share these secrets at the time, we would cherish that moment and share it with family and friends at a later date.

Being behind the scenes, we rarely saw celebrities, although there was one exception. To cover holiday, I had a week when I was duty night chef. It was a different experience than working during the day. Most of our night chores were completing mise en place and preparing food for late or early arrivals. Our guests could ask for anything from a full English breakfast to evening dinner, depending upon where they had just flown in from.

You never knew how many other chefs would be working; sometimes it was one chef on their own and occasionally they would be joined by a couple of other chefs who decided to work through the night to get ahead. Wayne Bosworth would occasionally be buzzing around somewhere in the kitchen, not because he was told to be there, just because he wanted to be there recreating and inventing dishes.

Wayne was there a couple of the evenings that I was working. To me it felt like a little safety net knowing that he was flickering in the background doing something. He would always in his busy night walk past you, asking if you were OK or giving you advice on certain prep you were doing. I liked that a lot about Wayne; some of the others found it annoying or nosey, but I found it quite comforting to have his knowledge nearby.

It was around midnight on one particular day. Most of the chefs and sous chefs had left, including Wayne, when suddenly my friend Giuseppe, the night waiter, came bursting into the kitchen asking for one of the sous chefs and I asked if I could help.

"Si si," said Giuseppe in his broad Italian accent. "Liza Minnelli is on her way back from the London Palladium where she's been performing tonight, and she wants to eat with her entourage."

I asked him how long she would be. After being informed he thought it would be another 10 to 15 minutes, I felt my stress levels rise. 'Oh my god. Liza Minnelli. 14 to 20 people want to eat now...' I started to panic. Even though the night menu was limited, it was a lot of work for one person to prepare food for this number of people. It was the same stress for Giuseppe as he was working on his own at the front of house and had to look after room service as well.

He said once they arrived, he would find out what they wanted to eat and let me know immediately.

Half an hour went by, and I heard nothing. I carried on with some of the chores that I had to do. It was approaching around 12.45am. I was working near to the sauce and fish section so I could be near to the restaurant entrance, when suddenly a head appeared from behind the swinging doors from the restaurant.

A tall, elegant lady looked straight at me and asked me whether there were any Italian chefs working there tonight. I paused for a moment and was struck dumb, slightly starstruck when I realised that it was Liza Minnelli herself standing in front of me, short dark hair, heavy make-up, dressed in a shiny, glittery silver dress, a shawl wrapped around her neck, with a big smile and her strong perfume wafting through the kitchen. Wow. She was the most glamorous woman I'd ever seen.

Before I could say anything, Giuseppe was right next to her, and they started to speak away in their mother tongue. After about 10 minutes he came across to me and told me that she wanted something Italian.

He read off some Italian dishes to me. At the time I wasn't very familiar with the dishes I was hearing, but I did know she mentioned spaghetti a couple of times. There were two Italian lads working in the veg section that night. They were peeling and turning vegetables, so I brought them both back up into the kitchen and Giuseppe explained to them what he needed. I also got him to explain to me what it was as I had the key to the refrigerators and the dry stores.

My excitement took over from my panic. They wanted to have spaghetti Napoli style which is basically spaghetti with tomato sauce, and they asked for a few other dishes. The young lads both got on with the preparation and started shouting away at one another in Italian. I assisted where I could and I felt a little bit useless, considering that I was in charge of night shift and I had two Italian chaps who were both second commis and spoke very little English bossing me around to grab ingredients, but I didn't mind. At least they were helping me out, saving me from making a spectacle of myself.

After about 35 to 40 minutes, between all four of us we created mini-Italian cuisine and asked Giuseppe to take the food out into the restaurant. "Ciao, bellissima," he thanked us. The two Italian chefs felt very proud of themselves; they were doing something that they totally understood, and they did extremely well. I was very grateful too.

I'll never forget that evening because it isn't very often that a celebrity would come into a kitchen and request that sort of food, and to also find the time to come and thank us afterwards, which she did with a big gleaming white smile. That was my first time of being close to such a famous person, so I was chuffed to bits!

We had spent about an hour and a half preparing their meal, but it was worth it. The rest of the night flew by and as the breakfast chef arrived, I couldn't keep the excitement to myself and shared my experience with him as he was getting his eggs together. He was smiling and acknowledging what we were saying, although I don't think he really cared. He was more concerned about breakfast and how many covers he was going to have rather than my celebrity experience.

Normally, a chef would leave around 7am after a night shift, but this day I wanted to share the experience with as many people as possible. Dave Sharland was the first sous chef to arrive and I told him how the event had a bit of glamour to it, and he congratulated us on coping so well.

We had also replenished most of the stuff that we used from different sections and still managed to get the stocks passed (through muslin to strain them to make the sauces for the next day), the Italians got their vegetables done and I got other things sorted out too. So, all in all it was a brave, successful evening. I was leaving to go home around 8.45 that morning and Chef already knew all about it. He stopped me and asked me how I had coped and I explained it was a bit of a shock and he congratulated me on a job well done.

That morning I bounced out of there feeling on top of the world and couldn't wait to tell my mother who I had met the previous night and cooked for, although I was unsure if she would believe me. The great thing about working in hotels like The Savoy is you get to meet great people and cook for them. I knew I was going to sleep when I got home; I was absolutely knackered.

INGREDIENTS FOR SUCCESS

I wasn't the type of guy to get starstruck, as I loved cooking for anyone, but when you would cook for a celebrity, you had something you could brag about. When you cooked for the rich and famous, it made you feel like a star yourself. As for meeting a celebrity, this was the icing on the cake.

They would often be singing or acting in the evening, which meant they would always be eating pretty late, which is similar to the world of a chef. We would grab food when things suddenly went quiet, and it didn't matter what time of day it was and I presume for the celebrities they would do the same.

Once again this is all part of the bright lights of The Savoy. If you get a chance to do something like this and then brag about it, then take any opportunity like this that you can.

CHAPTER 16:
THE NEW MENU

The menu would be changed around every three to four months. This was a hectic time in the kitchen. You would continue with the old menu, whilst keeping in the back of your head the knowledge that the new menu was coming into effect later that day or the next. It would mean that you would have to change your whole dishes, garnishes and mise en place.

For a few days, you would work 'à la minute' meaning that dishes would be prepared to order without having everything ready in advance. But with an à la carte menu, you didn't know what people were going to order; you had to guess what might happen depending upon what had happened in the past. It was a very stressful time, as you didn't want to create any waste or do any unnecessary work for a menu that was on its way out.

The old man liked to change everything at the same time. I think he believed once he got it out the way, the lads would take a few days to adapt and then it would get smoother. There were certain people who found this exciting. Bossie comes to mind once again as he thrived with the excitement of changing to new dishes. He would be running around the kitchen: chop-chop chop-chop, let's go, let's go, sweating and pulling his hair to one side under his hat and speaking with his heavy Yorkshire accent.

He would assist you as if he was the head chef of the kitchen. In some ways inside I think we all thought he was the working head chef. I'm not saying that the old man didn't work; Wayne was more like a sous chef, in my eyes anyway. You would create the dish on the plate that the old man had written out in a new menu, and he would give instructions to the sous chefs on how he wanted his plates to look. But it always seemed that it was Wayne who'd be tweaking and getting the old man's nod of approval.

The other sous chefs liked Wayne because he acted as the go-between person. It gave them time to focus, whilst Wayne went around tweaking all the things for the old man to make sure that every dish looked great.

Charming in his way, he would say things like... I think that's better looking like this or like that. You could come to a compromise but never felt threatened by him and he always had his camera at hand to take a picture of the final product. He wanted to be the one to present it to the Chef and run into the office with a plate to show him. You would look anxiously up at the office above the kitchen, to see the face of approval or disapproval. Nine times out of ten, he would stand up from his seat and look down at the plate and then look across at the section in the kitchen that they were talking about.

It was funny, most mornings you could tell exactly what mood he was in when he walked into his office. You would see him remove his coat and go into the back of his office where his changing room was, and if he came out and sat straight down at his desk you knew that was going to be a challenging day. If he was in a mild mood, he would put on his chef whites and come round the kitchen cracking jokes and being polite with everyone.

The day of the new menu came, and everybody was rushing around with last-minute adjustments and changing their garnishes. Everyone would be waiting for the first order and once that came and the new plate was ready to go out, there would be a gathering of people crowding around to see how each plate looked.

I felt a little bit sorry for the guys on the veg section because their dishes didn't vary very much. They just prepared the seasonal veg – haricot verts, broad beans, mangetout, glazed carrots, sauteed zucchini – and would often do a panache de legumes (a mixture of vegetables) in individual boat dishes. And there would be different types of potatoes, sauteed potatoes, Lyonnaise potatoes, pomme soufflée potatoes, mashed potatoes with nutmeg.

There were usually 8 to 10 varieties of vegetables and 4 or 5 different types of potato dishes. But the same format of prepping and blanching and having plates ready didn't change. They would have a couple of dishes that would be more technical but not many, hence why most of the lads who couldn't keep up with the pace would end up there. No one wanted to be on the veg section as it was intense, always on the go.

As I mentioned earlier, every section in that hotel provided for banqueting as well; veg was no exception. In fact, the veg section was twice as busy. In addition to providing vegetables for most of the dishes, they created vegetables to garnish, like petite salade, which supported most outlets in the kitchen, private rooms, banqueting and à la carte. Even cold starters would often have vegetables blanched and then garnished around the plate.

Gordon ran the veg section during my time at The Savoy. Gordon was a Northern Irish guy with a very strong accent, but he would always speak very quietly to you until you annoyed him, and then an outburst would come out and he would start banging pots and pans down telling you to move your ****. I experienced this while watching him a couple of times when I was taking stock out for the hot fish. It wasn't a very pretty sight for most of the lads on veg; it was like watching chickens running without heads as the orders kept tumbling in, so you could imagine how it was on the day of the new menu. They didn't have much to change but they still had to coordinate which vegetables were going to go with which plates and that was as demanding as the sauce for the fish.

Just imagine... someone ordered the Dover sole. The sole came with fleurons, puff pastry made into little fishes about an inch long, which came from the pastry. This would also involve the fish departments and saucier, and it would be served with sauteed potato, and then you'd call the larder to bring you a fresh garnish of salad for the side.

Five departments could be involved with one dish. There would be screaming from one person or another every two or three minutes as they coordinated retiring the old menu, and tempers would flare when things went wrong. The plate would arrive in the pass to be put together. They couldn't delay finishing the food on the pass, or they would get the evil eye from the Chef. Or something worse!

In fish, I always had an idea of what was going on with the new menu a few days in advance of the change. The old man would speak to me and tell me something like the sea bass was coming in rather than bream, how he wanted it cut and what the portion sizes were meant to be, which was an advantage. Once I knew the fish and exactly what was wanted, it was quite straightforward, still challenging though. I must say I enjoyed it when the menu changed. It was like another chapter of a book for me in learning more and understanding different dishes. We all wanted to learn new dishes and the old man did not deprive us of that even though it was stressful for the first week or so. Then we came back to the well-oiled machine that we had been before.

The food would turn out like it was on the picture pages of a book at the pass. I think we were 60% clear about what the food should look like and the other 40% was left up to the old man. He would browse, pause and say if he didn't like it. Then the sous chef would send it back and scream out to get you to do it again. There aren't many kitchens that I have worked in where we sent the food flowing out of the kitchen at such a rate and at such a high level but then that was all down to the team. I think teamwork means everything in kitchens all over the world and I've been fortunate enough to work in many kitchens around the world and none of them seem to have a push like this. It was a mean and angry kitchen but on the other hand charming and gentle all in one.

INGREDIENTS FOR SUCCESS

Having a new menu was like someone moving the furniture around in your house without your knowledge. I enjoyed the menu change, yes it could be strenuous and very busy, not in a service way but trying to get it right. In most professional kitchens, unless you are just opening, you don't get a chance to do dry runs.

It was an excellent time for understanding how to put your brakes on and how to control your order. The first few days of the new menu could be nerve-wracking but once you got into the swing of it, it was like learning something new again.

Learning anything new can put a new perspective on life and give you a new challenge to master.

CHAPTER 17:
THE GRIP

The Savoy had a grip on me. I would arrive at 6.30 some mornings. It was pitch dark in the winter.

On many occasions, the journey home to Turnpike Lane would be fruitless. If we finished too late, we missed the last tube home, and being tired and getting the night bus would often result in falling asleep and ending up in the wrong place. So, some days we slept on the locker room floor, often with a few of the other chefs including Giorgio Locatelli and Aubrey Williams.

We took off our old dirty whites, rolled them up and used them as a pillow and went to sleep in our clothes, only to wake up three hours later and put on clean whites and head back to the kitchen where the stoves that we had turned off earlier were still warm. We would fire them up again like we had never left and after a night of bad sleep because our minds were racing about the things we had to do, we just got straight back into it.

There were days where we could barely keep our head above water. It was relentless: the orders kept on coming, the new bookings kept on coming and you'd always be falling behind before the day was out. You would just about get through service for that one day before you were prepping into the small hours of the morning for the next. We often lost track of time as we didn't know what time of day it was. Through the few windows we did have in the old kitchen, it seemed to be dark all the time, whilst we worked in the sweatbox that was the main kitchen.

You would see a lot of chefs walking around like they'd been horse riding and with corn starch coming out of the back of their trousers. They had 'chef's arse'! This expression was for someone who had basically been sweating so much that they'd used corn starch to stop this sweat from going into the crease between their bum which became very sore after a while. I think we all suffered from it while we were there as the heat was so intense.

We also wore heavy steel toe capped boots that were issued to us when we first arrived at the hotel which had a strong grip on the soles to prevent slips in the kitchen. These boots took a toll on your feet. Imagine yourself in the kitchen – the temperature was always around 45 degrees Centigrade, 50 on some occasions, very hot, very sticky. As you can imagine as the hours passed by, your feet started sweating, causing blisters, and then there was the odour of wearing the boots for hours on end. And on the outside, the salt that's on the floor when the floor is being cleaned with detergent would mean that eventually these boots would give way. When they wore out, usually after around six months, you'd be issued with a new pair – free of charge of course. So we never ran out of shoes to wear.

Bossie told me early on, "You watch, those heavy boots they start off weighing 1lb and at the end of the day they're going to feel like they weigh 10lbs." He was right because normally by the end of the day most chefs were dragging their feet or taking their shoes off because their feet were aching.

You would be forgiven for thinking: Why would you work there? Why would you work all those hours? Why would you endure the heavy boots and the chef's arse?

Well, the experience was amazing; as I've already mentioned, the Chef used to always say that if you can work at The Savoy, you can work anywhere. That was very true. I found that out later on in life in other houses that I worked in, even my own restaurant, that it was never intense like this. The truth is we loved it; you were suddenly no longer work-shy and the heavy load seemed like a normal day.

My first year passed by like the blink of an eye. Normally when you worked at The Savoy, you would work on one section for six months and then be moved on to another section, but most of the ambitious chefs wanted to work on sauce and hot fish, as they were the two premier sections of the whole hotel. This is where you could show up at your best. Cold fish is such a vast section; there's so much to do and so many things to learn. It isn't a section I think where you can just spend six months and then move away from and I knew that the Chef knew that too.

He would often ask me if I was happy, and my response would be "Yes Chef". The advantage of learning how to prepare food to precision made you a better chef, and the more preparation you do, the less likely you are to go wrong. I love that way of thinking in the kitchen. I've watched many chefs over the years fall flat on their face who say they can cook but never prep properly. You couldn't blame the lads who looked down at you and thought that you couldn't cook, thinking that you only knew one thing, how to prep fish and do fish dishes, but I knew more than just fish as I mentioned earlier in the book.

When I worked under Frankie Manners at Belstead Brook, he taught me a lot of things about preparation and also how to plate food, and this ace card would always be in my pocket.

As chefs we never got to visit the front of the house very often unless we were cutting across the hallway to go to a function, but we knew it was there. We were basically like a swan with our legs underwater frantically working to make the front of house shine. I think I prefer that than being in the public all the time. I don't think I could smile all day.

In 1985 the hotel seemed to be winning everything I would read in the local rags. Chefs like Wayne Bosworth were coming back from Stuttgart where they went and won gold medals for the food that we displayed. He took on the position of night chef for a while and always had a camera around his neck. He would come and see me before the end of service in the evening and asked me if I had any fish from this dish or that dish that he could have. This was because he often worked late to create new dishes during the course of the night. Wayne loved it like it was some form of magic, that he could get everything done in the evening and still have time to create his dishes.

There were many chefs like this who wanted to just cook good food. There were bunches of different characters there. I sometimes wonder where they all are today, and I found some of them. I keep in touch with about four or five. I know where Giorgio is, I know where Aubrey is, Andrew Jordan and Graeme Watson. If only I had taken much more notice while we were there and got to know them all a lot better. But you've got to remember we were young lads around 17, 18 and 19, not much older.

I gave up my teenage years for a hot kitchen for a dream. When this comes calling you don't refuse, and we were the chosen few to wear that jacket with the big blue embroidery. It made me so proud. It was an ongoing thing that when you turned back up on a Monday morning after being off for the weekend you would take your dirty chef whites down to the linen room and change them for a set of clean, freshly pressed folded chequered trousers and chef jacket and apron and this would be important to you. Some of the most senior chefs would have about four or five jackets in their locker and you would wonder how they'd achieved that, but I don't think they could be bothered to be visiting the linen room every two days so they would end up with about five jackets in their lockers. There was a system to be maintained and pride and most of the chefs lived this to the letter.

INGREDIENTS FOR SUCCESS

Using the terminology, the grip is when you seem to have your whole day and night morphed into one and a week into a month. Often you would want to go home but you wouldn't because you were too busy. It's not like you didn't trust your staff, it was just because you were too busy and you didn't want to let the Chef or your lads down. This is when you must pull together; this is when you have to show your strength.

This has taught me a lot in life. When you're at your busiest you've got to grip together and see a way through. This is one of the strengths that I carry with me every day in my kitchens. We will not fail as long as we pull together.

CHAPTER 18:
MAKE OR
BREAK TIME

I was now moving into my second year and as a snake sheds its skin so did our kitchen brigade. Some senior members were moving on and some junior members were promoted. It was always sad to see someone that you really liked leaving but when they told you that they had been there three years before you and they were moving on, you would always wonder what you would be moving on to. What could be better than The Savoy?

Graeme Watson and Phil Mears were two likeable chefs. I remember when they left the hotel. Graham was on hot fish, and he'd been there longer than me. I was surprised he was leaving because he was the next in line to be the chef de partie of that section, but I think he'd done his time.

You see, when you work at The Savoy you can see when everything is coming to a head and your time has been spent. Graham wasn't that old. He must have been about easily 23 when he left, maybe younger. Phil was about the same age, but these guys had started a good year before me, so I understood they wanted a new challenge.

When most of the lads left, they never bragged about where they were going or what they were going to do next. They would tell the few that they were close to and keep it close to their chest. It felt like nearly every Friday there was someone leaving and every Monday another five to six people starting. It was like walking to the edge of a cliff. You would wonder when you were going to be at the edge, and you were going to leave, but I think deep inside we all knew that day when we would do it.

I was there when Bossie decided he was going to leave. It was very hard to tell how many days he was there because he worked so many different shifts, but you could always hear his voice even if you couldn't see him. I remember him telling me that he was going to leave. At that time, he was working as a sous chef, but I think his passion wanted to take him further. I would have loved to work with him on a one-on-one basis. I'd never seen someone with so much passion. He was ready to go on and do bigger things. The lads were always considerate to the people who had been there a long while and always wanted to give them a good send-off, and Bossie was no exception. Weeks after he left it still seemed a lot quieter, like a little bit of the energy had been zapped from the kitchen but just like the boys it kept ticking on; as the menus changed our positions changed.

I was now beginning to get itchy feet and wanted to move and change sections within the hotel. I didn't want to go to any other sections but fish or sauce. I covered larder a lot in my early days when I was at Belstead Brook and also covered veg there. It wasn't like there was anything new to learn there; I'd seen most of it as I worked on all areas when I first went there. I really didn't want to work in banqueting, even though Mr Jordan was quite a pleasant chap; it just seemed like it would be routine doing the same thing every day in bulk, so it only really left these two options.

I asked the old man if I could get a transfer to sauce or hot fish. As per usual, he used it as a bargaining tool. He said to me, "If you want to do that Michael, you can do me three months as a night chef, and I'll think about it." I was a little bit annoyed as I'd given him a long time consistently in cold fish. I found that very harsh and it wasn't fair to the sous chefs. There wasn't much I could do so I just kept my head down for the time being. I was learning a hell of a lot and I knew exactly what the hot fish was doing; every day I told myself that, and it was true to a point. I could step right into hot fish and continue.

It was shortly afterwards that my friend Noel came up to me, the one who lived in the same house as me alongside the waiter we met on our first day, John Laing. He said, "Mickey, I'm going to hand in my notice this Friday." I was shocked because we had started at the same time. We were both just getting into our second year, so I was surprised he wanted to leave.

He had done his year and Noel was the kind of guy who wanted to travel too. I was surprised when he told me that he might go to the Lygon Arms, which was a sister hotel in Worcestershire, literally on the doorstep of where he came from. I gave him a funny look when he told me this. It's a great hotel, but not so busy and not so big, but it still had the same standards so I could understand that.

The main time that was always considered make or break time was the Christmas season. Most of the chefs who were thinking of leaving would always try and do it before this season began. They'd feel trapped with everything coming at you during those two months with the full artillery of menus, from à la carte to banquet.

I must say it crept up on you. One minute it was the end of October, just busy with à la carte, and then the next minute banqueting would be all over you. It disrupted the kitchen with its high demands. Andrew Jordan would suddenly appear like Mr Benn from nowhere, with his clipboard in hand and going through all the things that he would be requiring from individual sections.

You could see the chefs de partie trying to reorganise themselves and delegating jobs to certain individuals in the kitchen of their department. The sous chefs were mingling and helping out. I would like to say that they did this all the time, but most of the time they would stay at arm's length except for the occasional few. The storm had arrived, and we all knew it. For the next seven to eight weeks, we ran at full capacity. Days off would be suspended and long hours would start, dark mornings and dark nights. You wouldn't see daylight. Our whole lives would be one big mess.

Each day would be a list of things to do, and we were just repeating ourselves as the weeks went on. Just keep working and accommodate the late parties that arrived. I think it was the Chef that was strongest and showed his leadership. You'd see him on occasions helping out in the larder, helping out in the distressed sections whilst still talking to people.

In cold fish it was a blur. I was so busy I didn't know if I was coming or going. I totally ignored the need for sleep just to get the job done. It was like everyone was coming at me from all directions. I was not only having to make sure that I had fish portions ready for à la carte but now on top of that I had to deal with parties myself, plating up cold starters and also preparing decorations of lobsters and crabs for the cold buffets, dismantled, cooked and put back together, displayed in the cages in which they were caught, but easy for people to eat.

We would have these massive mirrors, and I would have to dress them. I would cut the fish portions; the hot fish department would poach it in fish kettles. I would take it out of the kettle and peel all the skin off it and let it cool. Once it was cool, I would use thinly sliced cucumber and arrange it on the fish like it was scales, covering the whole fish. We would use egg yolks and mayonnaise to make a paste and put it into a piping bag and pipe it down the centre of the fish to make a spine. For hors d'oeuvres we would make tomato rousse, where we would blanch the tomatoes, take out all the flesh from the middle, and then using diced carrot, petit pois, turnips and other blanched vegetables, add mayonnaise and put them into the tomato. Then I'd have medallions of salmon, which would be covered in decorative scales too, and I'd decorate around the fish with garnishes to make the platter. Alongside this were mousses, terrines and en croûtes for both the à la carte menu and banquets.

The long days took their toll. I think the Chef could see this in his team but encouraged us to keep on going. This was almost at the end of November 1986. Approaching

December, it would be the big push, as the days rolled into one and the hotel got busier.

You could feel the hotel shaking with full capacity and then suddenly around the 19th and 20th December, you could start to see the end of the tunnel. By that time, you could finally start counting down how many parties and full restaurants you had left before everything would come to a grinding halt, as London would shut down for Christmas around the 23rd or 24th December.

By that time, we would be numb with exhaustion and working on automatic pilot. But as we approached the end point, order came back, there was less screaming and shouting and smiles started to appear on the lads' faces again.

Christmas was the one time of the year where we would get more than one day off in a row. Most of the lads who arrived from France, Germany, Switzerland and other European countries would be getting ready to go home and visit their families. They'd start talking about what they were going to be doing when they got back home to be with their families and enjoy Christmas.

Most of us British chefs knew that we would have to hold the fort whilst they were away. We would have skeleton brigades for the Christmas. You had a choice. The sous chef would tell us that we could have Christmas or New Year off; you couldn't have both. If they didn't like you, they just put you on the one that they needed. I didn't really care much for either as I wasn't much of a Christmassy person so I would rather stay in the kitchen and get through it once everything had calmed down.

Some of the lads who went off for holidays never returned. Although they said that they'd see us in a couple of weeks, you could see it in their eyes. Plus, they had their knives tucked under their arms and had left nothing in their lockers to be desired. They would take their Christmas break and their Christmas money, what belonged to them, and leave. I can quite understand that but at the same time I would be annoyed that they were cowards and wouldn't work their notice period.

Around the 4th and 5th January, when everyone started to return, you could see who was missing, but in good old Savoy form there were always new recruits ready to go. Like clockwork, on the Tuesday morning there was a new group of newbies arriving in the kitchen being despatched to departments.

It was very rare that I received many new recruits in my department. It wasn't one of the biggest; the maximum people in cold fish was a team of four or five. I would always end up with the trainees, the ones that come from the front of house to spend six weeks in the kitchen. I had Lisa, the daughter of Willie Bauer, the director, working for me for a couple of weeks along with her friend Fiona. Lisa and Fiona were dressed in jackets that were way too big for them. This was going to be hard work; I really had to work out what jobs to give the girls so they wouldn't get in my way, and I could carry on getting the day done.

Even though it was January, we were still a very busy hotel. We were picking up the tail end of late Christmas parties and starting off with seasonal menus, so the menus would be changing, and trial menus would be going out. By February the sous chef would start asking if you wanted to take a week off, because they had to get your holidays out of the way and were under a lot of pressure from Human Resources and the Chef to make sure it was done.

Sometimes you were bullied to take a week off. I really hated taking holiday because I knew that when I came back it was like starting all over again. As much as you could bark out your instructions and tell the lads what was going on there would always be someone running your department while you were away, and things would change. I'd take a week off in February, as it seemed to be the quietest month, well anyway for fish it was. I would try to relax and do other things that I wanted to do, but for some crazy reason I would miss the busyness of the hotel. I think it was running through my veins, what was going on at the hotel, what was happening during this week while I wasn't there. You would think any normal person wouldn't care but I'm sure most of us did when we worked there.

On the Monday when I arrived back after my week off, there was this big German chap in cold fish with wooden clogs on skipping around. The chef pulled me to one side. "Michael, I've given you someone to help in cold fish," he told me. I thanked him. "His name is Stephan and he's from Hamburg, he's a nice chap so be nice." This was one of the Chef's ways of saying be good, be kind to someone. His other expressions were 'always good food' and 'loving care'.

As I strolled into my section, I saw him. Moustache, blonde hair, broad shoulders, hands on hips and a big grin on his face. He introduced himself and we got to know each other. He had this funny laugh. He'd arrived about a week ago while I was off, along with another German guy called Thomas. The Chef had a connection in Hamburg in Germany and these two guys wanted to work here.

Stephan was always keen to bring new things from Germany into the section. He would say, "This is how we did it at the Vier Jahreszeiten in Hamburg…" I didn't know what the Vier Jahreszeiten meant, all I knew was that it was a hotel and yes this is how they did it there. So, I had to remind him this was the *Savoy* Hotel, and this is how we did it *here*.

He giggled and laughed and was eager to learn and watched. I was a bit concerned that the Chef brought him in as a chef de partie, and I wondered if he was trying to oust me. Was he trying to take over the kitchen with these German chefs? Although getting him up to speed with the larder, the cold fish and the hors d'oeuvres meant that he could work as a chef tournant, floating around from one department to another to help out.

Stephan soon picked things up and it took a lot of pressure off me because then I could get more time back to myself. I could leave work at a sensible time, and we had struck up a really good relationship. It was Stephan who started to talk to me about working abroad, how in Germany the kitchens ran with a similar structure, but the chefs were a lot older. Most of the chefs de partie in Germany were men of 50 years old. I was shocked, really, but chefs de partie is an important department. When you were in charge of a department where not even the sous chef could interfere with you, this was very different.

I was interested and spent many days asking him question after question about how things worked in Germany. I did fantasise about working in places abroad but never took it seriously until that moment.

"What do you plan to do when you leave here, Michael?" he said.

"I'm not really thinking about leaving," I replied.

"What, you want to stay here forever?"

He got me thinking. "Well not forever, but you know I like the job I do, and it might not be as rewarding as I want it to be, but I feel that I'm a part of a team here."

"Ah you have to feed them well," he said, and then with a big grin he would trek off to do something, then come back and continue the conversation. In fact, the whole month of February and March seemed a lot easier having someone that you could speak to on the same level and who didn't make mistakes.

He spent two months with me learning and then Stephan moved over to the larder, but he would occasionally pop in to help me out and have a chat. I also struck up a great friendship with his friend Thomas who was working in the hot kitchen with other lads, so I would casually browse through and see how he was settling in. If we got out in time and we ended up in the Coal Hole, our famous pub, we would chat about how things worked abroad.

I think I was making my mind up that my next move from The Savoy would be overseas. I didn't know where, but I knew there weren't any better hotels in London than The Savoy, so I didn't see the point in staying.

It was the famous book *Leading Hotels of the World* that changed everything for me. I got my hands on a copy and started looking at all of the top hotels. We were in there, of course, but then I noticed they had the Vier Jahreszeiten – the best hotel in Europe and number three in the world in those days, and the Mandarin Hotel in Hong Kong was the number one.

I would look at these pictures, staring at them for ages. I thought to myself, I should work at every single hotel in this book, starting off in Europe and go halfway around the world and learn all these languages. It was a little escape from my everyday chores as I watched a lot of the senior lads getting ready to depart.

I now realised that I was one of the senior lads in the hotel after 2½ years. Wow, did I really think I would be there that long? I had done the full year twice. I was halfway around again. Every month I knew exactly what was going to happen; the stress of a newbie had left me a long time ago. I felt like the fixtures and fittings and it seems that everywhere I walked in the hotel everyone knew who I was. Maybe because there weren't that many people of colour, so I was very easy to recognise and remember.

Most of my working days were between 12 to 15 hours but on this particular day I found myself leaving to go home around 4.30. Aubrey said to me, "I'm getting out of here, wait for me." As we got changed and ready to leave the hotel, we were all making comments about the fact that we'd never left this early in our lives. It was well deserved for the hours that we put in, but funnily enough we all felt guilty that we were leaving so early even though we could only put in the hours that were asked of us.

We all ended up in the Coal Hole pub. It was one of the few afternoons that I can really say, when you went outside your workplace and just socialised with the lads, that you got to know who they really were. Most of them were young guys like me who were just trying to get on with their career. That meant a lot back then and getting a good reference from where you worked was very important.

It was a great afternoon and there was a great bonding spirit among all the chefs who left early, sitting there drinking and talking, sharing ambitions of where we wanted to be in the next 5 to 10 years and also sharing all our gripes and grumps.

INGREDIENTS FOR SUCCESS

———————————

When you have your best team completed like a well-oiled machine you know that one day this so-called perfect team will change. No different at The Savoy. In my time many great chefs have come and gone but it's the guys who had the character that you miss most. This would normally leave a void, the guys that were screaming and shouting the loudest in service, the ones that would get the attention from the sous chefs. We had a lot of leaders in the kitchen, great leaders who have become amazing chefs themselves. What I'm trying to say is that from the coming and going great leaders are made. Future head chefs, Michelin chefs. Make your leadership matter so that you create the new leaders and this will take you far.

CHAPTER 19:
SAVOY, SAVOY

By late April 1987, everything came to a head. I had decided that today was the day when I was going to hand in my notice. I had been at The Savoy for a long time and the Chef would understand if I wanted to move on and broaden my experience.

During the morning, the Chef passed through cold fish a couple of times, but I couldn't pluck up the courage to tell him that I needed to speak to him. He would just bark out things that he needed me to do and if I had them ready. And in my usual way, I responded "Yes Chef!"

Around midday, he popped in and was sampling the terrine de Romilly from my section, standing right next to me, telling me it was the best one I'd made yet. I thanked him. And as he turned to walk away, I plucked up my courage. "Chef, can I see you later on after service?"

"As long as you're not after a pay rise again Michael," he retorted and left.

I'd never asked for a pay rise, but it was just his way of letting you know that you weren't going to get one. I smiled and carried on working. The first step had been taken and I started to think about what I was going to say to him when I gave him the letter that I had in my back pocket.

Around 3pm was when service normally went calm and most of the lads quickly rushed to the canteen to get the last few remnants that were left from lunch service. The kitchen was at its most deserted and everyone got five minutes to get themselves together. This was the perfect time to see the Chef who was normally sitting in his office flicking through the paperwork that had been left on his desk with a teapot and cup and saucer next to him.

I walked up to the office, and he looked up, saw me approaching and flagged me in. I still knocked on the door when I arrived. I walked up the three steps and I was in his office.

"What can I do for you, Michael?" Chef was always straight to the point. There was no other way to put it, so I blurted out that I wanted to resign.

He looked up from his papers, and his first response was to ask who had upset me. But there had been no one. "Everything is perfect," I responded. "I just feel like I've been here nearly three years. I've learned so much from you and I need to move on."

I placed the letter in front of him and he ignored it and looked up at me. "Go, is that all you have to do, come in here and waste my time today?" was his response.

"No Chef, but it's important."

With both his elbows on the desk and his fingers interlocked he looked at me with his head to one side. "Rubbish, I don't want to hear it, get out of my office." I paused for a moment and then I turned and left as if I had started a war.

As I walked back down through the kitchen, I saw him lifting the letter from his desk and, without even looking at it, he ripped it in two and just threw it into the bin. I couldn't believe he had just done that. I was in shock. I walked back into the cold fish and looked out of the window for a few moments.

Aubrey had seen me when I was in office and came through to the cold fish. "What happened, Mikey?" I quickly explained it to him, and he responded, "Oh shit, I was going to go and see him this afternoon as well." I I looked at Aubrey and wished him better luck than me and with that, he left me.

A little later on that afternoon, Dave Sharland, who was working on the late shift, came past to talk to me. "Afternoon Mickey, what's this I'm hearing about you?" I asked him what he had heard. "Well, the old man was just telling me that you have resigned."

"More like I tried to resign Dave. He threw my letter in the bin!" I responded.

Dave burst out laughing. He told me that the old man had done exactly the same to him when he had left the first time. And in fact, he did it to a lot of the lads, more likely the ones he didn't want to leave because he liked them. He advised me to give it a day or two, go back in, tell him again and that he was sure he'd come around. I heeded Dave's advice and as he left, he pinched one of my prawns that I had cooked for display.

As the evening service started, with its usual rush, it got quite busy specially for me. It seemed that cold fish was the flavour of the day and the section was a bit full on. Suddenly the Chef appeared at the entrance and looked me dead in the eye and started to give me shit. For an hour and a half, it didn't matter how fast we worked, or how many orders we completed, it felt like he was deliberately telling everyone to buy cold fish that night to get back at me for resigning earlier.

Normally the Chef would go home around 8.30pm but that night he stayed, just to make sure I got his wrath. And at 10pm he left, without his usual goodnight. I was truly in his bad books.

As I was cleaning down my section along with the lads, Aubrey came through to check I was OK and made me feel better. I felt guilty that it must have been me that had put him in a bad mood and asked how Aubrey got on when he went in with his resignation letter. It was pretty much the same as me; although he didn't rip it up and just put it in the bin, he did tell Aubrey to get out of the office.

In a way, I felt a little better but it was two of us who had resigned from the fish sections. As Aubrey leant against the fish counter he told me how service went at the front of the kitchen. The old man was sending everything back that night and was even giving the sous chef shit.

As he walked through, Dave put his hands on his hips and looked at the two of us. His hat was on one side, and he was sweating from helping out. "Why couldn't you two have done this another day when I wasn't doing the evening shift!" Dave always made light of a bad situation and we all just laughed and left the hotel.

The next morning, the Chef turned up like nothing had happened the night before. He walked through the kitchen greeting his brigade and also popped his head into the cold fish and greeted me too. I greeted him back with a steady look and then continued to work. Everyone had their head down and had very little to say to one another. I just got on with the job in hand. We all knew when it was a quiet kitchen it could kick off at any minute so it's just best to keep yourself to yourself.

As midday approached, I couldn't help but wonder whether I should go back into the Chef's office with another letter or just wait. Service came and went, and I couldn't really focus as it was bothering me, so I decided I would try again. I approached the Chef's office, a little bit nervous, more than the first time. I knocked on his door and he didn't respond. I knocked again. He said "Come in" and then saw it was me. "Michael, I don't have time for this nonsense. I'm very busy. You will have to wait."

I immediately turned and left his office. I walked back to my fish section, thinking 'What's the point? You give someone three years of your life and they can't give you two minutes.' I'd made up my mind and decided to speak to David Louth in the Human Resources department. So I waited until 3.30pm and went to see him.

I entered the office and asked for Mr Louth. The young lady behind the desk asked me if I had an appointment with him. I said no but it is important, and she asked me to take a seat. They were the same seats that I'd sat on three years earlier at my induction. Nothing had changed. They were all still doing the routine, the same job they seemed to enjoy because they were all smiling, but I am sure you would smile too if you were doing eight hours a day, a far cry from the hours we put in working in the kitchen.

After 10 minutes, Mr Louth came out of his office and asked how he could help me. I stared back a bit in shock, surprised that he knew my name and remembered who I was. I composed myself and then told him about the incident with Chef over the last 24 hours. He smiled and looked back at me and said, "Don't worry, I have a meeting with Anton tomorrow." I was surprised. I would not dare even call him Anton. "After the meeting I'll call you into the office and you can have your moment."

"Thank you," I said, feeling a little bit silly as I left the office, but it seemed that Mr Louth had experienced something like this before. Nevertheless, if he could get the Chef to accept my resignation I would be grateful.

As I walked back upstairs to the kitchen Giorgio came running up beside me. "You big black ****. I heard you're leaving. Yes, news travels fast, so were you going to tell me or not?"

"Of course I was going to tell you, but I wanted to tell the Chef first." Giorgio understood, especially since Aubrey gave him his notice on the same day. But chefs always wanted to know what you were going to do when you decided to leave, although he was surprised when I told him I didn't have a new job to go to. It probably sounded silly and reckless, but I did have a plan, I just didn't want to share it with them yet.

I arrived back at cold fish, and everyone was approaching me asking whether the news was true, and when I was leaving. I felt a little bit disappointed that the lads knew before the Chef had confirmed it, but I knew it would be happening anyway.

True to form, David Louth was in the Chef's office the next day for a meeting. I carried on working in cold fish and waited until I heard the call on the intercom from the Chef asking me to come to his office. I left the lads to continue with their work, laying out instructions just in case I was longer than was expected.

David was sitting to the right of Chef and they both greeted me and invited me to sit down, so I did. The Chef started the conversation: "Michael, what is this nonsense that you have to get David here to speak to me about your resignation?"

I was very blunt in my response, "Chef I've approached you twice about me resigning. Both times you've dismissed the situation, so I approached Mr Louth to ask him to assist me."

At this remark, the Chef giggled and David left the office and we continued our discussion. The Chef continued to speak to me about other things that had been going on in the kitchen, pointing people out and making light jokes about them, and then he got down to business.

He asked me why I wanted to leave. I had to think on my feet; I had to give him a reason, so it came out of my mouth that I wanted to work abroad.

He leant back into his chair and linked his fingers. "Where would that be?"

I told him about my conversation with Stephan and the great stuff he had told me about the Vier Jahreszeiten Hotel. The Chef sat there, and nodded his head. "Very nice hotel Michael, but it is not The Savoy," he responded.

"I know this Chef," I replied.

He pondered for a few seconds. "You will be missed, Michael," he said, and he accepted my resignation. I did wonder why he hadn't accepted it two days before. I felt sad and very happy at the same time. As I left the office I put my thumbs up towards Aubrey and walked back to the cold fish. I now had to find a new hotel to work in. I was planning exactly how I was going to do it. I had one month's notice to work. I knew it would be a tough month but I was excited and up for the challenge.

As the days and weeks flew past in a blur, I started to realise I was disconnecting myself from all the forthcoming parties that I wouldn't be involved in. All I could see was the middle of May when my last day would be. Up until that time I'd been looking for a new job and sending application letters.

Most of the lads thought I was on my way to Germany, and I liked it that way as it kept them from asking too many questions. It was going to feel strange not coming to this old girl anymore, not smelling the old bin food smells as you walked down the side of the hotel to the entrance.

I really hoped I'd made the right decision. It felt so inside. I had become an animal of habit for the last three years and in a way, I didn't want to become like a record artist who was only known for a one-hit wonder. It was a big world out there, an exciting one too, and other stories had been told to me by the French and German chefs who I had worked with and it just made me want to do it more. I would definitely need to improve my French or learn German, but I don't think I was too worried about that.

About a week before I left, there were new arrivals just like every Monday and Tuesday and for the first time I was given two of them. And I thought 'What shall I do with these newbies? They only have a week to experience me. Well I could teach them the skeleton of the section, how it works and what is expected.' I decided not to tell them that I was leaving. I think I was really harsh and tough with them. That whole week I just wanted them to get up to speed very quickly. Before I knew it, it was the Thursday – the day before I left.

I was the type of person who would normally say my goodbyes and go, but Aubrey and I were asked where we were going to have our leaving drinks. A lot of these guys had become like my brothers and sisters and I owed them that. Aubrey arranged something. He was good at things like that; he was well loved and liked in the kitchen by all and I think they were really sad to be losing him.

On my final Friday, I arrived at work as per usual. I went down to hand in my dirty whites and collect clean ones as I was still working, and I knew that we probably wouldn't be leaving there until around 4 or 5 in the evening. I approached the linen room and I told the linen lady I was going. She was shocked. I got changed and went upstairs. I felt like the load of the world had been lifted off my shoulders as I entered the kitchen. It was busy, no different than any other Friday, but it felt different to me because I knew I wouldn't be experiencing the Saturday night or the Sunday morning, or in fact the week to come.

Nothing seemed to bother me at all as the morning flew past and before I knew it, it was 3 o'clock in the afternoon. I was busy explaining some of the dishes to the newbies when John Wood came through and told me to come with him into the main kitchen. The older boys were clustered together; Aubrey was standing in the middle and John pushed me into the middle with him. Some of the older lads made speeches. This was weird because people left The Savoy all the time without any speeches. The lads all huddled round shaking our hands, and then John presented Aubrey and myself with engraved knives. My knife was engraved with 'To Mike, from the Savoy boys'. We were both in shock and stunned. In all the time that I'd been there I'd never seen the boys give presents to people who were leaving. I was truly touched, a little bit tearful, but I didn't show them.

This warm-hearted gesture from the Savoy boys told me I was one of them and always would be. I still keep in touch with some of the boys today after all my travelling success. These guys are unique, every single one of them. I've worked in many places but never had the unity or feeling of togetherness like The Savoy.

A few weeks later I was at Dover with my large rucksack, on my way to France.

INGREDIENTS FOR SUCCESS

Making the decision to leave a place like The Savoy was hard because I loved working there. But to grow is to be like a flower in a flowerpot and I now know after many years of working away from The Savoy that it was the correct thing to do. As much as you take on board all this knowledge of one of the world's most famous houses, to make it blossom, or should I say to make yourself blossom, you need experience from other places.

If The Savoy could have given me all the other experiences I gained from around the world I think I would have stayed. But it was with me all the time as I travelled and it was for this reason that I travelled, because it opened my eyes about my industry.

So remember wherever you work, it might be the beginning but it is never your end and it will always be with you. I still use a lot of The Savoy ways in my media, live cooking and training today but I have also embraced many other ways of doing things, even though it was The Savoy that led me to that path. Never forget where you come from and where you can go.

CHAPTER 20:
AFTER
THE SAVOY

Training at The Savoy was a stepping stone for so many of the young men and women who started their careers there. Many of these characters helped to shape my own future but many also went on to build amazing careers for themselves.

In doing the research for this book, I interviewed many of the chefs that I trained with back in the early days, those who I've kept in touch with and remained friends with ever since.

I must start with the Master – he who must be obeyed – the old man! Of course, Anton Edelmann was only 36 years of age when I was working with him, but he seemed like a god. Like so many of us, he started at The Savoy as a commis saucier in 1971 and he went on to the same job at the Hotel de la Paix in Paris for two years before embarking on his military service for his native Germany. Further spells followed in Hotel Bayerischer Hof in Munich, then the Dorchester, London, the Portman Intercontinental and launching the 'Ninety Park Lane' restaurant for the Grosvenor House Hotel and also the Restaurant Lorraine Paris. And of course, as Maitre Chef de Cuisiniers and Board Director at The Savoy Hotel from 1982 to 2003. Life didn't stop there, and his final last hoorah was as part owner and chef patron of Great Hallingbury Manor creating his own restaurant, 'Anton'.

You can see that with such a role model we all wanted to follow in his footsteps and gain experience throughout the country and the world and find our own special niche.

Aubrey Williams is a good friend even today. He left The Savoy to join a sister hotel, the Lygon Arms in Broadway, Worcestershire, spent some time at the Waterside Inn, Bray and then went to Australia in 1989. He worked at the Regent of Sydney as Chef

Saucier and gained the 'three hat' status, equivalent to three Michelin stars. Moves around Australia followed and in 1995 he won the Western Australia Chef of the Year. He opened his own restaurant, 'Truffles' in Victoria. There were further moves around the country and he stayed in Melbourne for some time before returning home to Jersey in 2015.

You remember John Wood in my narrative; we also lived together for some of our time at The Savoy. John and I worked together again for 18 months at the Vier Jahreszeiten in Hamburg. His career has taken him to Europe, Asia, South Africa and Dubai, working only in five-star establishments including the Mount Nelson, Cape Town, and the Island Shangri-la, Hong Kong. In the UK he also worked at the Dorchester and at Cliveden where he gained a Michelin star. His final executive chef position was at the seven-star Burj-al-Arab Hotel in Dubai.

Along the way he also collected four AAA Rosettes and 8 out of 10 in the Good Food Guide and 13th best restaurant in the world. He then became Food and Beverage Director and Executive Chef at the Grove Hotel Hertfordshire before setting up his own company, Kitchen CUT, which is a hospitality technology system operating in over 56 countries.

Brian Whiting worked all around the UK as a chef before he teamed up with Chris Hammond and formed Whiting and Hammond, an independent family business with the aim of taking run-down pubs and transforming them. By 2019 he had eight lovely places dotted around the southeast. During lockdown he took the opportunity to keep his pubs going, even working as a delivery driver for takeaways.

So many great chefs came via The Savoy. Graeme Watson ran the fine dining room at the Westin Hotel in Seattle at the grand age of 23. He also worked in Michelin-starred restaurants in London including Walton's and Inigo Jones. He also owned his own restaurant which he set up in a derelict cotton mill in the centre of Leicester for nine years and won his own accolades during that time. He is now the Operations Director for Wilson Vale Catering and has been the Vice Chairman of the Masterchefs of Great Britain since 2020.

And then there was 'Bossie'. Wayne Bosworth worked at The Savoy for three years before embarking on his further career. He worked for some time at Odette's in London before returning to his hometown of Sheffield to the Charnwood Hotel. In 1993 he opened a restaurant with his brother Jamie called 'Rafters'. The restaurant had a Bib Gourmand in the Michelin Guide and was a leading restaurant in Sheffield. Bossie died in a car accident in June 2000.

And what about me...

The days after The Savoy took me on a world tour. My journey continued at the George V, Paris, then the Vier Jahreszeiten in Hamburg. After Hamburg I went to the Angleterre in Copenhagen, then the Grand Hotel Regina in Switzerland, followed by the Grand Hotel Stockholm, the Capri Palace Italy, the Royal York Toronto, the Dorchester London, Mango Bay Island Barbados, Intercontinental Berlin, Soneva Fushi in the Maldives, the Mandarin Singapore, the Delta Palace Bangkok, and Simpsons Group of Cornhill London. Then I had my own restaurant in Blandford Street, London for 10 years – Michael Moore. I then opened Michael Moore Thirteen in Norway. I have also done a lot of media work in many of these countries as well as at the BBC in the UK.

Now I provide food and wine consultancy to food entrepreneurs and businesses across the world.

I could go on forever. But it all started at The Savoy, wanting to learn and share. Being a chef is unique; it is one of the few industries where you can take your skills all over the world and use them.

Because I love cooking and travel so much it has been a wonderful combination. My energy remains strong as does my willingness to learn.

But The Savoy for me was the start of a beautiful relationship with food and wine. I walk past it occasionally and smile and under my breath I say thank you.

Never be scared to live your dreams. You never know where they may take you...

GLOSSARY

General phrases

Hors d'oeuvres — (pronounced 'or-DERVS') The small one- or two-bite items that are served before dinner, usually accompanied by cocktails.

Mise en place — A French culinary phrase referring to the preparation of your section, or area, in a kitchen. It covers all of your equipment and ingredients.

Panné — To be coated in, for example when you coat your meat, fish, shellfish or vegetables in breadcrumbs. Examples would be recipes such as crispy, deep-fried mushrooms.

Terrine d'homard Romilly — A paté made with lobster and langoustine tails which was served with a lobster claw for decoration.

Kitchen sections

Potage — Where soups, noodles and pasta are prepared and cooked

Saucier — Responsible for the creation of sauces and also prepares all pan-fried and sautéed items

Poissonnier — Fish sauces, fish garnishes and cooked fish

Poissonnier froid — Cold fish preparation

Rôtisseur	Cooking of all red and white meat utilising a variety of cooking methods
Entremetier	Responsible for the preparation of dishes that do not involve meat, fish or seafood. This includes egg-based dishes, but primarily vegetables.
Larder	Cold kitchen
Boucherie	Preparation of meat and poultry
Patissier	Prepares all sweet items including desserts
Plonge	Washing up – pot wash (the most important section in the kitchen)
Brigade	The kitchen brigade system (brigade de cuisine) is a hierarchical system that delineates responsibility for each station in a professional kitchen. The system is attributed to Georges Auguste Escoffier, who first instituted it in the kitchen at London's Savoy Hotel.

Roles within the brigade

Executive chef	An executive chef is responsible for the successful management of a restaurant's kitchen. Their duties include designing menus, managing restaurant staff and organising financial budgets.
Head chef	(Chef de cuisine) Their principal function is to plan, organise and supervise the work of the kitchen.
Senior sous chef	The sous chef or underchef is the principal assistant of the head chef.
Sous chef	Works under the direction of the senior sous chef
Chef tournant	Talented chef who can work anywhere
Chef de partie	Heads of departments e.g. sauce or fish – a working cook in charge of a clearly defined section of activities within the kitchen.

First commis	Commis are the main 'backbone' of the kitchen. They are qualified and experienced to a good degree, but need more seniority before moving into the chef de partie position. They are trained cooks who have not yet reached full chef status.
Second commis	Works with the first commis
Trainee chefs	With each partie there will also be found apprentices or trainees who will be learning by helping in the practical day-to-day work of food preparation and cookery.
Maître d'	Restaurant manager
Kitchen porter (KP)	Without the KP no kitchen functions correctly. The kitchen porters are the unsung heroes in the kitchen. They make sure that everything is in the right place at the right time, and yes, that includes lifting and carrying. They must keep the kitchen clean so running round after the chefs, sweeping the floors, cleaning down, tidying up. And very importantly the washing up. The kitchen is quite hierarchical as you can see from the brigade and the porters are at the bottom but the chefs couldn't be without them!

ABOUT MICHAEL MOORE

Michael had hard-working parents, but his life was fairly dysfunctional in his younger years. As a black teenager it was hard to look to the future as there weren't that many options for people of colour. But Michael didn't want a labour-intensive type of job. He wanted a job that represented his growing character. His connections were drama, music and naturally food. The first two hadn't fully developed in their own right and it was nearly impossible for him to get into either of those industries. So his passion was food and that dictated his future direction. It stirred a few people in his final years at school as there were some who couldn't see the strength of his character and determination. His other two passions became his hobbies and entertainment, but cooking became his life.

His journey as you will see through this book and becoming a young chef led him into many exciting times with travels abroad. Meeting people and learning new cultures shaped his approach to cooking, enabling a diverse repertoire. His sense of fun and ability to make friends wherever he goes are amongst his greatest strengths. He lives by the motto that if you believe in yourself you can do anything. He was always ambitious and still is – there is more to come…

Milton Keynes UK
Ingram Content Group UK Ltd.
UKHW030135310823
427710UK00002B/15